# SOUP MAKER
## RECIPE BOOK

*150 Simple and Delicious Soup Maker Recipes, Healthy Life*

**Inna Volia**

# Table of Contents

INTRODUCTION ..... 8
Advice for a healthy life ..... 10
1-Creamy Potato Leek Soup ..... 11
2-Lentil Bacon Soup ..... 13
3-Creamy Chicken Soup ..... 15
4-Easy Carrot Soup ..... 17
5-Tasty Cauliflower Soup ..... 19
6-Butter Bean Soup ..... 21
7-Healthy Red Lentil Soup ..... 23
8-Lentil Mix Vegetable Soup ..... 25
9-Easy Tomato Lentil Soup ..... 27
10-Indian Lentil Soup ..... 29
11-Yellow Lentil Soup ..... 31
12-Spicy Lentil Carrot Soup ..... 33
13-Flavorful Lentil Carrot Soup ..... 35
14-Roasted Pepper Tomato Soup ..... 37
15-Chunky Onion Carrot Soup ..... 39
16-Lentil Squash Carrot Soup ..... 41
17-Nutritious Black Bean Soup ..... 43
18-Chicken Bean Soup ..... 45
19-Red Bean Tomato Soup ..... 47
20-Easy Carrot Green Bean Soup ..... 49
21-Butter Bean Carrot Soup ..... 51
22-Red Bean Turkey Soup ..... 53
23-Kale Bean Soup ..... 55
24-Chickpea Bean Soup ..... 57
25-Yummy Chicken Noodle Soup ..... 59
26-Asian Prawn Soup ..... 61
27-Pasta Vegetable Soup ..... 63
28-Flavorful Orzo Soup ..... 65
29-Cabbage Potato Soup ..... 67
30-Healthy Celeriac Soup ..... 69

31-Classic Chicken Noodle Soup ............................................................ 71
32-Parsnip Beans Soup ........................................................................... 73
33-Apple Potato Leek Soup ..................................................................... 75
34-Tasty Chicken Vegetable Soup ........................................................... 77
35-Creamy Broccoli Pumpkin Soup ........................................................ 79
36-Bacon Cabbage Soup ......................................................................... 81
37-Creamy Mushroom Soup ................................................................... 83
38-Delicious Minestrone Soup ................................................................ 85
39-Potato Bacon Soup ............................................................................. 87
40-Chili Chicken Soup ............................................................................ 89
41-Cheese Broccoli Soup ........................................................................ 91
42-Tomato Cabbage Soup ....................................................................... 93
43-Leek Mushroom Soup ........................................................................ 95
44-Cauliflower Broccoli Carrot Soup ..................................................... 97
45-Roasted Eggplant Soup ...................................................................... 99
46-Flavorful Tomato Soup .................................................................... 101
47-Creamy Tomato Soup ...................................................................... 103
48-Bacon Tomato Soup ......................................................................... 105
49-Parmesan Basil Tomato Soup .......................................................... 107
50-Creamy Squash Sweet Potato Soup ................................................. 109
51-Turkey Bean Soup ............................................................................ 111
52-Chicken Mushroom Soup ................................................................ 113
53-Creamy Mushroom Onion Soup ..................................................... 115
54-Thai Chicken Soup .......................................................................... 117
55-Chicken Sweet corn Soup ................................................................ 119
56-Thick & Creamy Pea Soup .............................................................. 121
57-Chili Squash Soup ............................................................................ 123
58-Delicious Asian Chicken Soup ........................................................ 125
59-Root Vegetable Soup ....................................................................... 127
60-Simple Courgette Leek Soup ........................................................... 129
61-Vegan Potato Soup ........................................................................... 131
62-Creamy Leek Potato Soup ............................................................... 133
63-Tomato Cabbage Soup ..................................................................... 135
64-Zucchini Coconut Soup ................................................................... 137

65-Cheesy Spinach Soup ... 139
66-Healthy Spinach Soup ... 141
67-Easy Mint Pea Soup ... 143
68-Pea Bacon Soup ... 145
69-Easy Broccoli Soup ... 147
70-Parmesan Asparagus Soup ... 149
71-Cashew Asparagus Soup ... 151
72-Vegan Celery Soup ... 153
73-Brussels Sprouts Cauliflower Soup ... 155
74-Creamy Carrot Sprout Soup ... 157
75-Cinnamon Squash Apple Soup ... 159
76-Bean Veggie Minestrone Soup ... 161
77-Blue Cheese Brussels Sprout Soup ... 163
78-Caprese Soup ... 165
79-Healthy & Easy Tomato Soup ... 167
80-Vegan Kale Miso Soup ... 169
81-Creamy Potato Soup ... 171
82-Broccoli Lemon Soup ... 173
83-Versatile Vegetable Soup ... 175
84-Lime Sweet Corn Soup ... 177
85-Corn Veg Soup ... 179
86-Mexican Corn Soup ... 181
87-Garlic Corn Soup ... 183
88-Apple Pumpkin Soup ... 185
89-Apple Ginger Squash Soup ... 187
90-Apple Parsnip Soup ... 189
91-Pear Parsnip Soup ... 191
92-Squash Pear Soup ... 193
93-Celery Pear Soup ... 195
94-Artichoke Tomato Soup ... 197
95-Herb Tomato Artichoke Soup ... 199
96-Tomato Eggplant Soup ... 201
97-Lebanese Eggplant Soup ... 203
98-Spicy Pumpkin Soup ... 205

99-Spicy Sweet Potato Soup ..................................................... 207
100-Poblano Corn Soup ........................................................... 209
101-Spicy Cabbage Soup............................................................ 211
102-Nutmeg Pumpkin Soup....................................................... 213
103-Cauliflower Cheese Soup ................................................... 214
104-Cauliflower Chicken Soup.................................................. 216
105-Curried Cauliflower Soup .................................................. 218
106-Cheesy Cauliflower Soup ................................................... 220
107-Herb Asparagus Soup ........................................................ 222
108-Nutritious White Bean Soup.............................................. 224
109-Spinach Green Lentil Soup ................................................ 226
110-Spicy Carrot Soup................................................................ 228
111- Curried Zucchini Soup ...................................................... 230
112-Creamy Cauliflower Soup .................................................. 231
113-Cheesy Broccoli Soup ......................................................... 233
114-Coconut Garlic Mushroom Soup....................................... 235
115-Cabbage Coconut Soup ...................................................... 237
116-Avocado Soup ...................................................................... 239
117-Broccoli Avocado Soup ...................................................... 241
118-Chicken Taco Soup ............................................................. 243
119-Almond Broccoli Cheese Soup .......................................... 245
120-Healthy Chickpea Lentil Soup .......................................... 247
121-Roasted Pepper Soup.......................................................... 249
122-Chickpea Chicken Soup..................................................... 251
123-Cheesy Asparagus Soup .................................................... 253
124-Basil Celery Soup................................................................ 255
125-Vegan Mushroom Soup..................................................... 257
126-Coconut Celery Soup ......................................................... 259
127-Celery Broccoli Soup ......................................................... 261
128-Pepper Zucchini Soup ....................................................... 263
129-Tomato Carrot Soup.......................................................... 265
130-Healthy Veggie Soup.......................................................... 267
131-Chicken Enchilada Soup.................................................... 269
132-Sweet Potato Soup..............................................................271

133-Asian Pepper Soup ............................................................. 273
134-Pesto Zucchini Soup .......................................................... 275
135-Yummy Chicken Tomato Soup ......................................... 277
136-Chili Chicken Soup ............................................................. 279
137-Vegan Bean Soup ............................................................... 281
138-Cannellini Bean Soup ........................................................ 283
139-Tasty Carrot Peanut Butter Soup ..................................... 285
140-Veggie Chicken Soup ......................................................... 287
141-Chicken Rice Noodle Soup ................................................ 289
142-Pumpkin Spice Cauliflower Soup ..................................... 291
143-Chicken Kale Soup ............................................................. 293
144-Mexican Chicken Soup ...................................................... 295
145-Chunky Tomato Cabbage Soup ......................................... 297
146-Italian Cabbage Soup ........................................................ 299
147-White Bean Carrot Soup ................................................... 301
148-Curried Cauliflower Soup ................................................. 303
149-Healthy Tomato Green Bean Soup .................................. 305
150-Almond Green Bean Soup ................................................ 307
Conclusion .................................................................................. 309

# INTRODUCTION

Soup is a delicious and healthy hot meal that comes with various health benefits. It is made up of healthy and nutritious vegetables. A bowl of soup before a meal helps to reduce your food cravings and prevents overeating, plus it also ensures you stay energized throughout the whole day. To make a healthy and delicious soup you need very few ingredients. If you are on a diet and want to lose or maintain your body weight, soup is one of the healthiest choices for you. Soups are not only delicious, they also contain essential vitamins such as vitamin A, vitamin C, vitamin D, nutrients and fibers. It helps to boost your energy levels because it contains carbohydrates, proteins, and nutrients. Soups are easily digested and provide a steady energy source to your body. There is even a research study that proves that consumption of tomato soup will help to reduce the risk of cancer because it contains antioxidants and lycopene. Soup is a delicious and highly nutritious meal made up of simple ingredients such as fresh vegetables and fruits, meat, grains herbs, and spices. There are various types of soups made up of a variety of ingredients. You can have soup as a healthy snack between your meals. Soups are consumed as a classic first course in western culture which is served before the meal. It helps to maintain your body weight because it contains low calories and is rich in essential nutrients. Another study even shows that miso and soy-based soups help to reduce the risk of breast cancer.

A soup maker is an amazing kitchen gadget for soup lovers to make soup easily at home. The modern soup maker appliance comes with an inbuilt blender which will help to chop and mix ingredients while making soup. The traditional soup-making process is time-consuming, as preparation from chopping to simmering takes lots of time. Instead of this, the modern soup maker is easy to operate and reduces your time, stress and cleaning process. A soup maker looks like a large kettle or thermos flask which has a heating element at the bottom of the flask to cook food. The flask lid has long blending blades that reach into the flask. These blending blades are used to blend food to achieve a smooth texture after the food is cooked. The soup maker takes around 20 to 30 minutes of time to make a delicious and healthy soup. Most of the soup makers offer cold blending functions that help you to make your favorite smoothie and shakes.

This soup maker recipe book helps you to learn different types of globally inspired soup maker recipes. The recipes written in this book are easily prepared and given with exact cooking time.

# Advice for a healthy life

- A healthy life is one which helps you to improve your health and well being. There are many different ways for you to live a healthy lifestyle. These include consuming healthy foods, eating soup before a meal and maintaining your body mass.
- Research shows that people who consume soup before a meal have smaller waists and lower weights than those people who don't eat soup. A bowl of soup taken before a meal will help to increase fullness and decrease hunger.
- A bowl of soup before a meal will improve your digestion system. Healthy soups are full of fiber content which helps to prevent constipation problems and improves your digestive system.
- A bowl of soup before a meal improves your blood circulation. Soups contain a large number of green vegetables which are enriched with antioxidants. These antioxidants have inflammatory and detoxifying properties which help to remove the excess toxins from your blood and improve your body's blood circulation.
- To improve the level of vitamins, minerals, and nutrients into your body, you should consume soup daily. It contains plenty of vitamin A, vitamin C, vitamin D, magnesium, potassium, iron minerals, and essential nutrients.
- A daily bowl of soup helps to keep you healthy and improves your cardiovascular health. Soup is enriched with vitamin C, minerals and antioxidants which provide protection to your coronary arteries which supply blood to heart muscles.

# 1-Creamy Potato Leek Soup

**Time: 30 minutes**

**Serve: 4**

**Ingredients:**

- 2 leeks, sliced
- 4 cups vegetable stock
- 1 tsp garlic, minced
- 1 onion, chopped
- 3/4 lb potato, peeled and diced
- 1 tbsp butter
- Pepper
- Salt

**Directions:**

- Melt butter in a saucepan over medium heat.
- Add onion and sauté for 2 minutes.
- Add garlic and leek and sauté for 2-3 minutes or until leek is softened.

- Transfer sautéed onion, garlic, and leek to the soup maker.
- Add remaining ingredients and stir well.
- Seal soup maker with lid and cook on smooth mode.
- Season soup with salt and pepper.
- Serve and enjoy.

**Nutritional Value (Amount per Serving):**

- Calories 136
- Fat 3.2 g
- Carbohydrates 24.9 g
- Sugar 4.3 g
- Protein 3.2 g
- Cholesterol 8 mg

## 2-Lentil Bacon Soup

**Time: 25 minutes**

**Serve: 4**

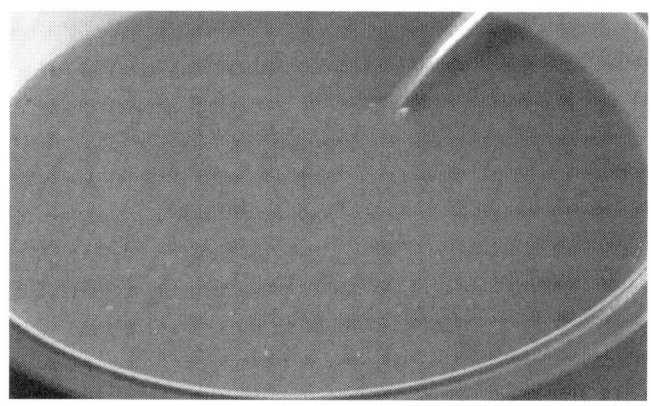

**Ingredients:**

- 4 cup vegetable stock
- 1/2 cup carrot, chopped
- 1 potato, peeled and chopped
- 7 oz split red lentils, rinsed
- 1/2 cup onion, chopped
- 3 bacon slices, chopped
- 1 tbsp olive oil
- Pepper
- Salt

**Directions:**

- Heat oil in a pan over medium heat.
- Add onion and bacon and sauté for 3-4 minutes.
- Transfer sautéed onion and bacon to the soup maker.
- Add remaining ingredients and stir well.

- Seal soup maker with lid and cook on smooth mode.
- Season soup with salt and pepper.
- Serve and enjoy.

**Nutritional Value (Amount per Serving):**

- Calories 332
- Fat 10.1 g
- Carbohydrates 41 g
- Sugar 3.3 g
- Protein 19.6 g
- Cholesterol 16 mg

# 3-Creamy Chicken Soup

**Time: 32 minutes**

**Serve: 4**

## Ingredients:

- 2 chicken breasts, cut into bite-size pieces
- 2 chicken stock cubes
- 1/2 tsp dried thyme
- 2 cups of water
- 2/3 cup milk
- 2 celery stalks, sliced
- 1 carrot, peeled and diced
- 2 leeks, sliced
- 1 onion, diced
- 2 medium potatoes, peeled and diced
- 1 tbsp olive oil
- Pepper
- Salt

## Directions:

- Heat oil in a pan over medium-low heat.
- Add onion and chicken and sauté until onion is softened.
- Add celery, carrot, leek, onion, potatoes, and thyme and cook for 10 minutes or until chicken is cooked.
- Transfer pan mixture to the soup maker.
- Add stock cubes, milk, and water to the soup maker and stir well.
- Seal soup maker with lid and cook on smooth mode.
- Season soup with salt and pepper.
- Serve and enjoy.

## Nutritional Value (Amount per Serving):

- Calories 313
- Fat 10.1 g
- Carbohydrates 30 g
- Sugar 6.8 g
- Protein 25.8 g
- Cholesterol 69 mg

# 4-Easy Carrot Soup

**Time: 30 minutes**

**Serve: 4**

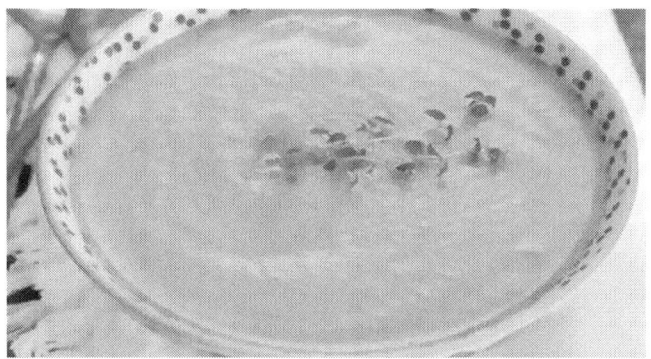

**Ingredients:**

- 1 3/4 lbs carrots, chopped
- 4 cups vegetable stock
- 1 tsp coriander powder
- 1 medium onion, chopped
- 1 tbsp olive oil
- 1/4 cup fresh coriander, chopped
- Pepper
- Salt

**Directions:**

- Heat oil in a pan over medium heat.
- Add onion and sauté until onion is softened.
- Transfer sautéed onion to the soup maker.
- Add carrots, stock, and coriander powder to the soup maker and stir well.
- Seal soup maker with lid and cook on smooth mode.

- Season soup with salt and pepper.
- Garnish with fresh coriander and serve.

**Nutritional Value (Amount per Serving):**

- Calories 128
- Fat 3.6 g
- Carbohydrates 23 g
- Sugar 11.6 g
- Protein 2.3 g
- Cholesterol 0 mg

# 5-Tasty Cauliflower Soup

**Time: 30 minutes**

**Serve: 6**

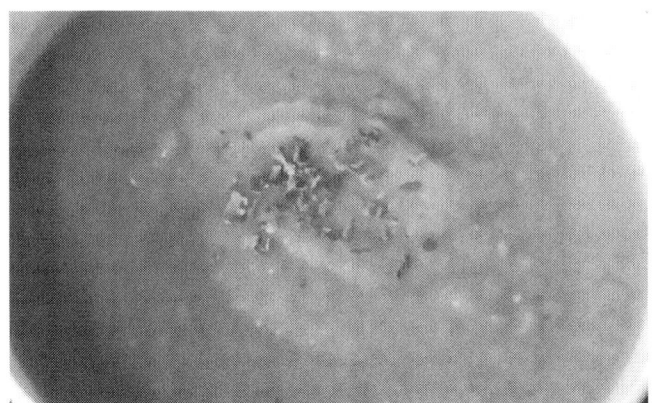

## Ingredients:

- 1 medium cauliflower head, cut into florets
- 1/2 tsp dried parsley
- 1/2 tsp dried mix herbs
- 1 cup of water
- 1/4 cup yogurt
- 1 bell pepper
- 1 small butternut squash, peeled and chopped
- 1 onion, chopped
- Pepper
- Salt

## Directions:

- Add all ingredients except yogurt into the soup maker.

- Seal soup maker with lid and cook for 25 minutes on blend mode.
- Add yogurt and stir well.
- Season soup with salt and pepper.
- Serve and enjoy.

**Nutritional Value (Amount per Serving):**

- Calories 76
- Fat 2 g
- Carbohydrates 11.9 g
- Sugar 5.4 g
- Protein 4.4 g
- Cholesterol 1 mg

# 6-Butter Bean Soup

**Time: 30 minutes**

**Serve: 4**

**Ingredients:**

- 14 oz can butter beans
- 3 1/4 cups vegetable stock
- 1/2 tsp coriander powder
- 10 oz passata
- 1/2 cup split red lentils, rinsed
- 1/2 tsp garlic, crushed
- 1 medium onion, chopped
- 1 tbsp olive oil
- Pepper
- Salt

**Directions:**

- Heat oil in a pan over medium heat.
- Add onion and sauté until softened. Add garlic and sauté for 30 seconds.

- Transfer sautéed onion and garlic to the soup maker.
- Add remaining ingredients and stir well.
- Seal soup maker with lid and cook on smooth mode.
- Season soup with salt and pepper.
- Serve and enjoy.

**Nutritional Value (Amount per Serving):**

- Calories 240
- Fat 4.6 g
- Carbohydrates 36.2 g
- Sugar 2.2 g
- Protein 12.5 g
- Cholesterol 0 mg

## 7-Healthy Red Lentil Soup

**Time: 26 minutes**

**Serve: 4**

### Ingredients:

- 2 cups split red lentils, rinsed and soaked in water for 30 minutes
- 1 medium onion, chopped
- 4 cups vegetable stock
- 1 cup potatoes, peeled and diced
- Pepper
- Salt

### Directions:

- Add all ingredients into the soup maker and stir well.
- Seal soup maker with lid and cook on smooth mode.
- Season soup with salt and pepper.
- Serve and enjoy.

**Nutritional Value (Amount per Serving):**

- Calories 382
- Fat 1.2 g
- Carbohydrates 67.1 g
- Sugar 4.3 g
- Protein 26.1 g
- Cholesterol 0 mg

# 8-Lentil Mix Vegetable Soup

**Time: 30 minutes**

**Serve: 4**

**Ingredients:**

- 1 lb mixed vegetables, chopped
- 3 1/4 cups vegetable stock
- 1/2 tsp garlic, minced
- 1/4 cup lentils
- 1/4 tsp allspice mix
- Pepper
- Salt

**Directions:**

- Add all ingredients into the soup maker and stir well.
- Seal soup maker with lid and cook on smooth mode.
- Season soup with salt and pepper.
- Serve and enjoy.

**Nutritional Value (Amount per Serving):**

- Calories 89
- Fat 0.5 g
- Carbohydrates 16.2 g
- Sugar 0.8 g
- Protein 5.1 g
- Cholesterol 0 mg

# 9-Easy Tomato Lentil Soup

**Time: 26 minutes**

**Serve: 6**

**Ingredients:**

- 1/2 cup red lentils, rinsed and soaked in water for 30 minutes
- 1/4 tsp dried mix herbs
- 1 vegetable stock cube
- 2 tbsp tomato puree
- 1 large carrot, chopped
- 1 tsp garlic, sliced
- 1 large onion, chopped
- 5 large tomatoes, chopped
- 4 cups of water
- Pepper
- Salt

**Directions:**

- Add all ingredients into the soup maker and stir well.
- Seal soup maker with lid and cook on smooth mode.
- Season soup with salt and pepper.
- Serve and enjoy.

**Nutritional Value (Amount per Serving):**

- Calories 161
- Fat 0.9 g
- Carbohydrates 36.1 g
- Sugar 11.2 g
- Protein 9.2 g
- Cholesterol 0 mg

# 10-Indian Lentil Soup

**Time: 26 minutes**

**Serve: 5**

**Ingredients:**

- 3/4 cup red lentils, rinsed and soaked in water for 30 minutes
- 1 vegetable bouillon cube
- 1 red chili, chopped
- 1 cup cherry tomatoes
- 1 carrot, peeled and chopped
- 1 tbsp fresh ginger, minced
- 1 tsp garlic, minced
- Pepper
- Salt

**Directions:**

- Add all ingredients into the soup maker.
- Add water to the soup maker up to the max mark.
- Seal soup maker with lid and cook on smooth mode.

- Season soup with salt and pepper.
- Serve and enjoy.

**Nutritional Value (Amount per Serving):**

- Calories 120
- Fat 0.5 g
- Carbohydrates 21.1 g
- Sugar 2.3 g
- Protein 8.1 g
- Cholesterol 0 mg

# 11-Yellow Lentil Soup

**Time: 26 minutes**

**Serve: 5**

## Ingredients:

- 1 cup split yellow lentils, rinsed and soaked in water for 1 hour
- 1 cup of water
- 1 1/2 tsp oregano
- 1 tsp chili powder
- 2 tsp ginger garlic paste
- 1 medium onion, chopped
- 1 large carrot, peeled and chopped
- 14 oz can tomatoes
- Pepper
- Salt

## Directions:

- Add all ingredients into the soup maker and stir well.
- Seal soup maker with lid and cook on smooth mode.

- Season soup with salt and pepper.
- Serve and enjoy.

## Nutritional Value (Amount per Serving):

- Calories 180
- Fat 1 g
- Carbohydrates 32.4 g
- Sugar 5.2 g
- Protein 11.5 g
- Cholesterol 0 mg

# 12-Spicy Lentil Carrot Soup

**Time: 26 minutes**

**Serve: 4**

**Ingredients:**

- 1 1/4 lbs carrots, peeled and chopped
- 1/2 cup milk
- 2 vegetable stock cubes
- 4 cups of water
- 3/4 cup red lentils, rinsed and soaked in water for 30 minutes
- 1 1/2 tsp cumin seeds
- 1/4 tsp red chili flakes
- 1 tbsp olive oil

**Directions:**

- Heat oil in a pan over medium heat.
- Once the oil is hot, add cumin seeds and red chili flakes and fry until cumin seeds crackle.

- Add carrots into the pan and stir everything well. Transfer to the soup maker.
- Add remaining ingredients to the soup maker and stir well.
- Seal soup maker with lid and cook on smooth mode.
- Season soup with salt and pepper.
- Serve and enjoy.

**Nutritional Value (Amount per Serving):**

- Calories 238
- Fat 4.9 g
- Carbohydrates 38 g
- Sugar 9.1 g
- Protein 11.8 g
- Cholesterol 0 mg

# 13-Flavorful Lentil Carrot Soup

**Time: 26 minutes**

**Serve: 4**

**Ingredients:**

- 1/2 lb red lentils, rinsed and soaked in water for 30 minutes
- 1 tbsp fresh lemon juice
- 2 tbsp fresh coriander, chopped
- 1 onion, chopped
- 1 sweet red pepper, chopped
- 2 large carrots, peeled and chopped
- 1/2 tsp paprika
- 1/2 tsp coriander powder
- 1 tsp cumin powder
- 1 tsp garlic, minced
- 4 cups vegetable stock
- Pepper
- Salt

## Directions:

- Add lentils, onion, red pepper, carrots, paprika, coriander powder, cumin powder, garlic, stock, pepper, and salt into the soup maker.
- Seal soup maker with lid and cook on smooth mode.
- Add lemon juice and stir well.
- Season soup with salt and pepper.
- Garnish with chopped coriander and serve.

## Nutritional Value (Amount per Serving):

- Calories 248
- Fat 1 g
- Carbohydrates 44.3 g
- Sugar 6.4 g
- Protein 16.2 g
- Cholesterol 0 mg

# 14-Roasted Pepper Tomato Soup

**Time: 1 hour 10 minutes**

**Serve: 6**

**Ingredients:**

- 9 medium tomatoes, halved
- 3 cups vegetable stock
- 1 tbsp vinegar
- 1 tbsp olive oil
- 5 garlic cloves, peeled
- 2 onions, diced
- 1 large sweet red pepper, diced
- Pepper
- Salt

**Directions:**

- Preheat the oven to 400 F/ 200 C.
- Place sweet red pepper, garlic, onion, and tomatoes on a baking tray.
- Drizzle with oil and vinegar.
- Bake in preheated oven for 45 minutes.

- Transfer roasted sweet red pepper, garlic, onion, and tomatoes to the soup maker.
- Add stock, pepper, and salt and stir well.
- Seal soup maker with lid and cook on smooth mode.
- Season soup with salt and pepper.
- Serve and enjoy.

**Nutritional Value (Amount per Serving):**

- Calories 82
- Fat 2.9 g
- Carbohydrates 13.4 g
- Sugar 7.8 g
- Protein 2.6 g
- Cholesterol 0 mg

# 15-Chunky Onion Carrot Soup

**Time: 38 minutes**

**Serve: 4**

## Ingredients:

- 6 medium onions, diced
- 1 tsp thyme
- 1/2 tsp dried mixed herbs
- 1 1/2 tsp chives
- 2 tbsp yogurt
- 4 celery sticks, diced
- 4 medium carrots, peeled and diced
- Pepper
- Salt

## Directions:

- Add all ingredients into the soup maker and stir well.
- Seal soup maker with lid and cook on chunky mode.
- Season soup with salt and pepper.
- Serve and enjoy.

**Nutritional Value (Amount per Serving):**

- Calories 104
- Fat 0.4 g
- Carbohydrates 23.4 g
- Sugar 11.1 g
- Protein 3.1 g
- Cholesterol 0 mg

# 16-Lentil Squash Carrot Soup

**Time: 26 minutes**

**Serve: 2**

## Ingredients:

- 1/2 lb butternut squash, peeled, deseeded, and chopped
- 2 tbsp red lentils, rinsed
- 1 vegetable stock cube
- 2 cups vegetable stock
- 2 carrots, peeled and chopped
- 1 medium onion, chopped
- Pepper
- Salt

## Directions:

- Add all ingredients into the soup maker and stir well.
- Seal soup maker with lid and cook on smooth mode.
- Season soup with salt and pepper.
- Serve and enjoy.

**Nutritional Value (Amount per Serving):**

- Calories 149
- Fat 0.7 g
- Carbohydrates 42.5 g
- Sugar 12.3 g
- Protein 5.8 g
- Cholesterol 0 mg

# 17-Nutritious Black Bean Soup

**Time: 30 minutes**

**Serve: 4**

## Ingredients:

- 14 oz can black beans
- 2 sweet potatoes, peeled and chopped
- 3 cups vegetable stock
- 1/2 tsp cayenne pepper
- 1/2 tsp cumin powder
- 1 tsp garlic, minced
- 1 carrot, peeled and chopped
- 1 onion, chopped
- 1 tbsp olive oil
- Pepper
- Salt

## Directions:

- Heat oil in a pan over medium heat.
- Add onion and sauté for 2 minutes. Add garlic and sauté for 30 seconds.
- Transfer sautéed onion and garlic to the soup maker.
- Add remaining ingredients and stir well.
- Seal soup maker with lid and cook on smooth mode.
- Season soup with salt and pepper.
- Serve and enjoy.

## Nutritional Value (Amount per Serving):

- Calories 235
- Fat 4.2 g
- Carbohydrates 43.7 g
- Sugar 3.6 g
- Protein 7.3 g
- Cholesterol 0 mg

# 18-Chicken Bean Soup

**Time: 38 minutes**

**Serve: 4**

**Ingredients:**

- 14 oz tomato passata
- 2 cups chicken stock
- 1 tsp Italian seasoning
- 14 oz can butter beans, drained
- 1 onion, chopped
- 1 cup soup pasta shells
- 2 chicken breasts, cooked and shredded
- 1 tsp olive oil
- Pepper
- Salt

**Directions:**

- Heat oil in a pan over medium heat.
- Add onion and sauté until onion is softened.
- Transfer sautéed onion to the soup maker.

- Add remaining ingredients and stir everything well.
- Seal soup maker with lid and cook on chunky mode.
- Season soup with salt and pepper.
- Serve and enjoy.

**Nutritional Value (Amount per Serving):**

- Calories 350
- Fat 7.6 g
- Carbohydrates 35.8 g
- Sugar 22.8 g
- Protein 33.8 g
- Cholesterol 62 mg

# 19-Red Bean Tomato Soup

**Time: 38 minutes**

**Serve: 4**

## Ingredients:

- 14 oz can tomatoes, chopped
- 14 oz can kidney beans, rinsed and drained
- 1 1/2 cups water
- 1/4 cup wheat bulgur
- 1 tbsp tomato puree
- 1/2 tsp paprika
- 1/2 tsp dried basil
- 1 onion, diced
- 2 vegetable stock cubes
- 1/2 tsp garlic, minced
- Pepper
- Salt

## Directions:

- Add all ingredients into the soup maker and stir well.
- Seal soup maker with lid and cook on chunky mode.
- Season soup with salt and pepper.
- Serve and enjoy.

## Nutritional Value (Amount per Serving):

- Calories 169
- Fat 0.3 g
- Carbohydrates 33.4 g
- Sugar 5.5 g
- Protein 8.4 g
- Cholesterol 0 mg

# 20-Easy Carrot Green Bean Soup

**Time: 33 minutes**

**Serve: 2**

## Ingredients:

- 2 cups green beans, diced
- 2 cups carrot, diced
- 2 tbsp fresh parsley, chopped
- 1 cup vegetable stock
- Pepper
- Salt

## Directions:

- Add all ingredients into the soup maker and stir well.
- Seal soup maker with lid and cook on chunky mode.
- Season soup with salt and pepper.
- Serve and enjoy.

## Nutritional Value (Amount per Serving):

- Calories 84
- Fat 0.2 g
- Carbohydrates 19.4 g
- Sugar 7.3 g
- Protein 3.2 g
- Cholesterol 0 mg

# 21-Butter Bean Carrot Soup

**Time: 26 minutes**

**Serve: 4**

**Ingredients:**

- 1 1/4 lbs carrots, peeled and chopped
- 1 tsp coriander powder
- 2 vegetable stock cubes
- 4 cups of water
- 1 onion, chopped
- 14 oz can butter beans, rinsed and drained
- Pepper
- Salt

**Directions:**

- Add all ingredients into the soup maker and stir well.
- Seal soup maker with lid and cook on smooth mode.
- Season soup with salt and pepper.
- Serve and enjoy.

**Nutritional Value (Amount per Serving):**

- Calories 159
- Fat 0.9 g
- Carbohydrates 31.2 g
- Sugar 8.1 g
- Protein 6.6 g
- Cholesterol 0 mg

## 22-Red Bean Turkey Soup

**Time: 33 minutes**

**Serve: 4**

**Ingredients:**

- 1 cup can red beans, rinsed and drained
- 1/2 lb ground turkey, crumbled
- 1/2 tsp dried oregano
- 2 tsp chili powder
- 1 onion, chopped
- 4 oz can green chilies, diced
- 1 cup can tomatoes, crushed
- 2 cups chicken stock
- Pepper
- Salt

**Directions:**

- Add all ingredients into the soup maker and stir well.
- Seal soup maker with lid and cook on chunky mode.
- Season soup with salt and pepper.

- Serve and enjoy.

**Nutritional Value (Amount per Serving):**

- Calories 157
- Fat 5.6 g
- Carbohydrates 12.5 g
- Sugar 2.9 g
- Protein 16.1 g
- Cholesterol 46 mg

# 23-Kale Bean Soup

**Time: 30 minutes**

**Serve: 5**

**Ingredients:**

- 2 cups kale, tough stalks removed
- 4 cups vegetable stock
- 14 oz can butter beans, drained and rinsed
- 1 potato, peeled and cubed
- 1/2 tsp garlic, minced
- 1 onion, chopped
- 1 leek, chopped
- 1 tbsp olive oil
- Pepper
- Salt

**Directions:**

- Heat oil in a pan over medium heat.
- Add garlic and onion and sauté for 2-3 minutes.
- Transfer sautéed garlic and onion to the soup maker.
- Add remaining ingredients and stir well.

- Seal soup maker with lid and cook on smooth mode.
- Season soup with salt and pepper.
- Serve and enjoy.

**Nutritional Value (Amount per Serving):**

- Calories 156
- Fat 3.5 g
- Carbohydrates 25.4 g
- Sugar 2.5 g
- Protein 6.3 g
- Cholesterol 0 mg

# 24-Chickpea Bean Soup

**Time: 30 minutes**

**Serve: 4**

**Ingredients:**

- 1 1/4 cup canned chickpeas, rinsed and drained
- 1 1/4 cup canned black beans, rinsed and drained
- 3 cups vegetable stock
- 1/2 bell pepper, diced
- 1/2 tsp cumin powder
- 1 jalapeno pepper, chopped
- 2 tbsp fresh lime juice
- 1 tsp garlic, minced
- 1 onion, chopped
- 1 tbsp olive oil
- Pepper
- Salt

## Directions:

- Heat oil in a pan over medium heat.
- Add onion and garlic and sauté for 2-3 minutes.
- Transfer sautéed onion and garlic to the soup maker.
- Add remaining ingredients and stir well.
- Seal soup maker with lid and cook on smooth mode.
- Season soup with salt and pepper.
- Serve and enjoy.

## Nutritional Value (Amount per Serving):

- Calories 223
- Fat 4.9 g
- Carbohydrates 38.1 g
- Sugar 3.6 g
- Protein 9.1 g
- Cholesterol 0 mg

# 25-Yummy Chicken Noodle Soup

**Time: 33 minutes**

**Serve: 6**

## Ingredients:

- 1/2 lb chicken, cooked and shredded
- 1/2 lb potatoes, peeled and cubed
- 1 chicken stock cube
- 3 oz noodles, broken into pieces
- 4 cups chicken stock
- 1 tbsp flour
- Pepper
- Salt

## Directions:

- Add all ingredients into the soup maker and stir well.
- Seal soup maker with lid and cook on chunky mode for 28 minutes.
- Season soup with salt and pepper.
- Serve and enjoy.

**Nutritional Value (Amount per Serving):**

- Calories 116
- Fat 1.9 g
- Carbohydrates 11.2 g
- Sugar 1 g
- Protein 12.9 g
- Cholesterol 33 mg

# 26-Asian Prawn Soup

**Time: 30 minutes**

**Serve: 4**

**Ingredients:**

- 3 1/2 lbs fresh prawns
- 1 cup fish stock
- 1/4 cup yogurt
- 1 lime, juiced
- 1 tsp ginger garlic paste
- 1/2 tsp paprika
- 1/2 tbsp curry powder
- 1/2 tsp mixed spice
- 1 tsp coriander powder
- 1 small onion, chopped
- 1 red pepper, chopped
- Pepper
- Salt

## Directions:

- Add all ingredients into the soup maker and stir well.
- Seal soup maker with lid and cook on blend mode for 25 minutes.
- Season soup with salt and pepper.
- Serve and enjoy.

## Nutritional Value (Amount per Serving):

- Calories 521
- Fat 7.9 g
- Carbohydrates 13.3 g
- Sugar 3.6 g
- Protein 93.5 g
- Cholesterol 837 mg

# 27-Pasta Vegetable Soup

**Time: 35 minutes**

**Serve: 4**

**Ingredients:**

- 3/4 cup orzo pasta
- 2 1/4 cup water
- 2 vegetable stock cubes
- 14 oz can tomatoes, chopped
- 1 tsp garlic, chopped
- 1 cup frozen peas
- 1/2 tsp turmeric powder
- 1/4 tsp garam masala
- 1 tbsp curry powder
- 1 red pepper, diced
- 1/4 tsp chili powder
- 1 tsp ginger garlic paste
- 1 onion, chopped
- 1 tbsp olive oil
- Pepper
- Salt

## Directions:

- Heat oil in a pan over medium heat.
- Add onion, pepper, garlic, and ginger garlic paste and sauté until onion is softened. Transfer into the soup maker.
- Add remaining ingredients into the soup maker and stir well.
- Seal soup maker with lid and cook on chunky mode for 25 minutes.
- Season soup with salt and pepper.
- Serve and enjoy.

## Nutritional Value (Amount per Serving):

- Calories 191
- Fat 5 g
- Carbohydrates 31.5 g
- Sugar 8 g
- Protein 7 g
- Cholesterol 18 mg

# 28-Flavorful Orzo Soup

**Time: 30 minutes**

**Serve: 4**

**Ingredients:**

- 3/4 cup orzo pasta
- 2 chicken stock cubes
- 1 tbsp curry powder
- 1 tbsp ginger, grated
- 1 small apple, cored and diced
- 1 tsp garlic, chopped
- 2 celery sticks, diced
- 1 onion, diced
- 1 carrot, diced
- 4 cups of water
- 1 tbsp olive oil
- Pepper
- Salt

## Directions:

- Heat oil in a pan over medium heat.
- Add onion, ginger, and garlic and sauté until onion is softened.
- Transfer sautéed onion, ginger, and garlic to the soup maker.
- Add remaining ingredients to the soup maker and stir well.
- Seal soup maker with lid and cook on chunky mode for 25 minutes.
- Season soup with salt and pepper.
- Serve and enjoy.

## Nutritional Value (Amount per Serving):

- Calories 166
- Fat 4.6 g
- Carbohydrates 26.8 g
- Sugar 8.3 g
- Protein 4.2 g
- Cholesterol 18 mg

## 29-Cabbage Potato Soup

**Time: 35 minutes**

**Serve: 4**

**Ingredients:**

- 1 cup cabbage, shredded
- 14 oz can tomatoes, chopped
- 14 oz can chickpeas, rinsed and drained
- 2 1/4 cups water
- 1 potato, peeled and diced
- 1 green chili, chopped
- 1/2 tsp garlic, minced
- 1 tsp ginger, grated
- 1 onion, diced
- 1 tsp turmeric
- 1/2 tsp coriander powder
- 1 tsp cumin powder
- 1/2 tsp mustard seeds
- 2 vegetable stock cubes
- 1 tbsp olive oil

## Directions:

- Heat oil in a pan over medium heat.
- Once the oil is hot, add mustard seeds and let them pop for 30 seconds.
- Add onion, ginger, garlic, and green chili and sauté until onion is softened. Transfer into the soup maker.
- Add remaining ingredients into the soup maker and stir well.
- Seal soup maker with lid and cook on chunky mode for 25 minutes.
- Serve and enjoy.

## Nutritional Value (Amount per Serving):

- Calories 233
- Fat 5.2 g
- Carbohydrates 40.8 g
- Sugar 5.8 g
- Protein 7.7 g
- Cholesterol 0 mg

# 30-Healthy Celeriac Soup

**Time: 30 minutes**

**Serve: 4**

### Ingredients:

- 3/4 lb celeriac, peeled and diced
- 3/4 cup yogurt
- 2 1/4 cups water
- 2 vegetable stock cubes
- 1/2 tsp fennel seeds
- 1 potato, peeled and diced
- 1 onion, diced
- 1 leek, sliced
- 1 cup celery, sliced
- Pepper
- Salt

### Directions:

- Add all ingredients except yogurt into the soup maker and stir well.

- Seal soup maker with lid and cook on smooth mode for 21 minutes.
- Add yogurt and stir well.
- Season soup with salt and pepper.
- Serve and enjoy.

**Nutritional Value (Amount per Serving):**

- Calories 136
- Fat 1.2 g
- Carbohydrates 25.7 g
- Sugar 7.3 g
- Protein 5.8 g
- Cholesterol 3 mg

# 31-Classic Chicken Noodle Soup

**Time: 38 minutes**

**Serve: 4**

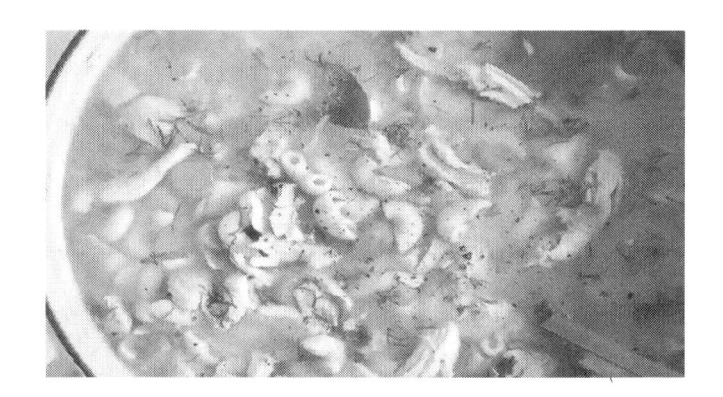

**Ingredients:**

- 2 chicken breasts, diced into small chunks
- 1.5 oz egg noodles
- 1 tsp dried rosemary
- 1 tbsp ginger, grated
- 2 chicken stock cubes
- 3 3/4 cups water
- 1/2 tsp garlic, minced
- 2 carrots, peeled and diced
- 1/4 cup spring onions, sliced
- 2 celery sticks, sliced
- 1 tbsp olive oil
- Pepper
- Salt

## Directions:

- Heat oil in a pan over medium heat.
- Add chicken and cook until brown.
- Transfer chicken to the soup maker. Add remaining ingredients to the soup maker and stir well.
- Seal soup maker with lid and cook on chunky mode for 28 minutes.
- Season soup with salt and pepper.
- Serve and enjoy.

## Nutritional Value (Amount per Serving):

- Calories 206
- Fat 9.2 g
- Carbohydrates 8.6 g
- Sugar 2 g
- Protein 21.7 g
- Cholesterol 66 mg

# 32-Parsnip Beans Soup

**Time: 60 minutes**

**Serve: 4**

## Ingredients:

- 1 1/4 lbs parsnips, peeled and quartered
- 1 celery stick, chopped
- 2 vegetable stock cubes
- 2/3 cup milk
- 14 oz can cannellini beans, rinsed and drained
- 1 tsp cumin seeds
- 1/2 tsp turmeric powder
- 1/2 tsp garlic, minced
- 1 onion, chopped
- 1 potato, peeled and diced
- 2 cups of water
- 1 tbsp olive oil
- Pepper
- Salt

## Directions:

- Preheat the oven to 350 F/ 180 C.
- Place parsnip, garlic, and onion on a baking tray and drizzle with oil. Season with salt and pepper.
- Roast in preheated oven for 30 minutes.
- Transfer roasted parsnip, garlic, and onion to the soup maker.
- Add remaining ingredients to the soup maker and stir well.
- Seal soup maker with lid and cook on smooth mode for 21 minutes.
- Season soup with salt and pepper.
- Serve and enjoy.

## Nutritional Value (Amount per Serving):

- Calories 282
- Fat 5.2 g
- Carbohydrates 54 g
- Sugar 10.3 g
- Protein 10.1 g
- Cholesterol 3 mg

# 33-Apple Potato Leek Soup

**Time: 26 minutes**

**Serve: 4**

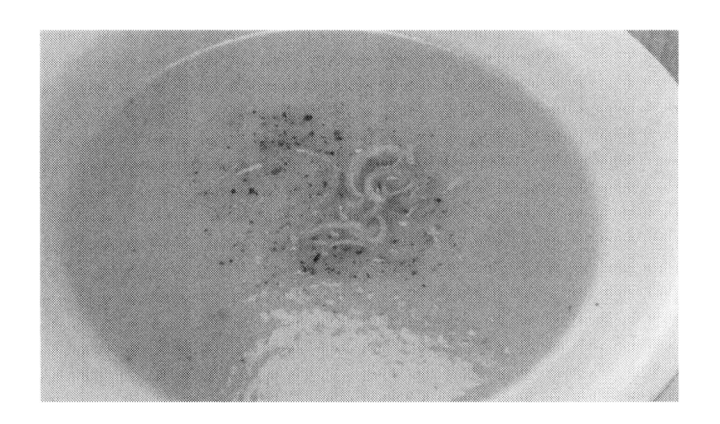

**Ingredients:**

- 1 1/2 cups potato, peeled and chopped
- 2 leeks, sliced
- 1 cup apple, diced
- 1/2 tsp dried rosemary
- 1/2 tsp mustard powder
- 1/8 tsp cayenne pepper
- 3 3/4 cups water
- 1 garlic clove, peeled
- 2 vegetable stock cubes
- Pepper
- Salt

## Directions:

- Add all ingredients into the soup maker and stir well.
- Seal soup maker with lid and cook on smooth mode for 21 minutes.
- Season soup with salt and pepper.
- Serve and enjoy.

## Nutritional Value (Amount per Serving):

- Calories 87
- Fat 0.6 g
- Carbohydrates 20.1 g
- Sugar 7.8 g
- Protein 1.8 g
- Cholesterol 0 mg

# 34-Tasty Chicken Vegetable Soup

**Time: 38 minutes**

**Serve: 4**

**Ingredients:**

- 1 cup chicken breasts, cooked and diced
- 1/8 tsp liquid stevia
- 1 tsp coriander powder
- 1/2 lemon juice
- 1 tsp turmeric powder
- 1 red chili, sliced
- 1 cup mushrooms, sliced
- 2 chicken stock cubes
- 4 cups of water
- 1 tbsp ginger, grated
- 1 tsp garlic, minced
- 1 1/4 cup butternut squash, peeled and diced
- 1/4 cup spring onion, sliced
- Pepper
- Salt

## Directions:

- Add all ingredients except lemon juice into the soup maker and stir well.
- Seal soup maker with lid and cook on chunky mode for 28 minutes.
- Add lemon juice and stir well.
- Season soup with salt and pepper.
- Serve and enjoy.

## Nutritional Value (Amount per Serving):

- Calories 106
- Fat 3 g
- Carbohydrates 8.5 g
- Sugar 1.7 g
- Protein 11.8 g
- Cholesterol 31s mg

# 35-Creamy Broccoli Pumpkin Soup

**Time: 26 minutes**

**Serve: 4**

**Ingredients:**

- 3 1/2 cups broccoli, chopped
- 4 cups of water
- 2 vegetable stock cubes
- 1 tsp paprika
- 1 green chili, chopped
- 1 tsp ginger, grated
- 1 onion, chopped
- 1 cup pumpkin, diced
- Pepper
- Salt

## Directions:

- Add all ingredients into the soup maker and stir well.
- Seal soup maker with lid and cook on smooth mode for 21 minutes.
- Season soup with salt and pepper.
- Serve and enjoy.

## Nutritional Value (Amount per Serving):

- Calories 68
- Fat 0.8 g
- Carbohydrates 14.3 g
- Sugar 4.7 g
- Protein 3.5 g
- Cholesterol 0 mg

# 36-Bacon Cabbage Soup

**Time: 30 minutes**

**Serve: 4**

**Ingredients:**

- 1/4 cabbage, sliced
- 5 bacon slices, cooked and chopped
- 2 vegetable stock cubes
- 4 cups of water
- 2 1/2 cups potatoes, peeled and diced
- 1 tsp dried rosemary
- 1 garlic clove, minced
- 1 celery stick, sliced
- 1 carrot, diced
- 1 onion, diced
- 1 tbsp olive oil
- Pepper
- Salt

## Directions:

- Heat oil in a pan over medium heat.
- Add onion to the pan and sauté until softened. Add garlic and sauté for 30 seconds.
- Transfer sautéed onion and garlic to the soup maker.
- Add remaining ingredients except bacon to the soup maker and stir well.
- Seal soup maker with lid and cook on smooth mode for 21 minutes.
- Add bacon and stir well.
- Season soup with salt and pepper.
- Serve and enjoy.

## Nutritional Value (Amount per Serving):

- Calories 250
- Fat 13.8 g
- Carbohydrates 20.6 g
- Sugar 3.2 g
- Protein 11.2 g
- Cholesterol 26 mg

# 37-Creamy Mushroom Soup

**Time: 30 minutes**

**Serve: 4**

**Ingredients:**

- 6 cups mushrooms, chopped
- 2 cups of water
- 2 cups of vegetable stock
- 1 tsp vinegar
- 1 tsp thyme
- 2 celery sticks, chopped
- 1 potato, peeled and chopped
- 1 tsp garlic, minced
- 2 onions, diced
- 1 tbsp olive oil
- Pepper
- Salt

## Directions:

- Heat oil in a pan over medium heat.
- Add onion and garlic and sauté until onion is softened. Transfer to the soup maker.
- Add remaining ingredients to the soup maker and stir well.
- Seal soup maker with lid and cook on smooth mode for 21 minutes.
- Season soup with salt and pepper.
- Serve and enjoy.

## Nutritional Value (Amount per Serving):

- Calories 116
- Fat 4 g
- Carbohydrates 17.5 g
- Sugar 5.1 g
- Protein 5.2 g
- Cholesterol 0 mg

# 38-Delicious Minestrone Soup

**Time: 38 minutes**

**Serve: 4**

**Ingredients:**

- 1 1/4 cups courgettes, diced
- 1 tbsp basil
- 3/4 cup pasta, break into pieces
- 2 celery sticks, sliced
- 1 onion, diced
- 2 carrots, peeled and diced
- 2 cups tomatoes, chopped
- 2 vegetable stock cubes
- 1 tbsp olive oil
- Pepper
- Salt

## Directions:

- Heat oil in a pan over medium heat.
- Add onion, celery, and carrots and sauté until onion is softened. Transfer to the soup maker.
- Transfer remaining ingredients to the soup maker.
- Seal soup maker with lid and cook on chunky mode for 28 minutes.
- Season soup with salt and pepper.
- Serve and enjoy.

## Nutritional Value (Amount per Serving):

- Calories 153
- Fat 2 g
- Carbohydrates 24.6 g
- Sugar 5.9 g
- Protein 4.8 g
- Cholesterol 18 mg

# 39-Potato Bacon Soup

**Time: 30 minutes**

**Serve: 4**

## Ingredients:

- 1 3/4 cup potatoes, peeled and diced
- 4 strips of bacon sliced, cooked and chopped
- 2 vegetable stock cubes
- 2 1/2 cups water
- 1/2 cup milk
- 1 cup leek, sliced
- 1 onion, chopped
- 1 tbsp olive oil
- Pepper
- Salt

## Directions:

- Heat oil in a pan over medium heat.
- Add onion and cook until onion is softened.
- Transfer sautéed onion to the soup maker.

- Add remaining ingredients except bacon to the soup maker.
- Seal soup maker with lid and cook on smooth mode for 21 minutes.
- Season soup with salt and pepper.
- Serve and enjoy.

**Nutritional Value (Amount per Serving):**

- Calories 200
- Fat 11.5 g
- Carbohydrates 18.2 g
- Sugar 4.2 g
- Protein 7.9 g
- Cholesterol 18 mg

# 40-Chili Chicken Soup

**Time: 38 minutes**

**Serve: 4**

**Ingredients:**

- 1 cup chicken, cooked and shredded
- 3 1/4 cup chicken stock
- 2 tbsp lime juice
- 1/2 tsp cumin powder
- 1 1/2 chili, chopped
- 1 garlic clove, chopped
- 14 oz passata
- 1 onion, chopped
- 1 tbsp olive oil
- Pepper
- Salt

## Directions:

- Heat oil in a pan over medium heat.
- Add onion, garlic, and chili and sauté until onion is softened. Transfer to the soup maker.
- Add remaining ingredients to the soup maker and stir well.
- Seal soup maker with lid and cook on chunky mode for 28 minutes.
- Season soup with salt and pepper.
- Serve and enjoy.

## Nutritional Value (Amount per Serving):

- Calories 251
- Fat 10.4 g
- Carbohydrates 22.8 g
- Sugar 3.3 g
- Protein 17.7 g
- Cholesterol 43 mg

# 41-Cheese Broccoli Soup

**Time: 30 minutes**

**Serve: 4**

## Ingredients:

- 2 cups broccoli, chopped
- 3 1/4 cup chicken stock
- 1 cup blue cheese, crumbled
- 1 potato, peeled and chopped
- 1 cup leek, sliced
- 1 celery stick, sliced
- 1 onion, chopped
- 1 tbsp olive oil
- Pepper
- Salt

## Directions:

- Heat oil in a pan over medium heat.
- Add onion and sauté until onion is softened.

- Transfer sautéed onion to the soup maker.
- Add remaining ingredients except cheese to the soup maker and stir well.
- Seal soup maker with lid and cook on smooth mode for 21 minutes.
- Top with crumbled cheese and season with salt and pepper.
- Serve and enjoy.

**Nutritional Value (Amount per Serving):**

- Calories 232
- Fat 14 g
- Carbohydrates 17.9 g
- Sugar 4 g
- Protein 10.6 g
- Cholesterol 25 mg

# 42-Tomato Cabbage Soup

**Time: 26 minutes**

**Serve: 4**

## Ingredients:

- 3/4 lbs of cabbage, chopped
- 1 3/4 cups hot water
- 1 vegetable stock cube
- 14 oz passata
- 1/2 tsp garlic, chopped
- 1 carrot, sliced
- 1 large onion, chopped
- 1 tbsp olive oil
- Pepper
- Salt

## Directions:

- Heat oil in a pan over medium heat.
- Add onion and garlic and sauté until onion is softened. Transfer to the soup maker.

- Add remaining ingredients to the soup maker and stir well.
- Seal soup maker with lid and cook on smooth mode for 21 minutes.
- Season soup with salt and pepper.
- Serve and enjoy.

**Nutritional Value (Amount per Serving):**

- Calories 108
- Fat 3.8 g
- Carbohydrates 21 g
- Sugar 6.8 g
- Protein 2.7 g
- Cholesterol 0 mg

## 43-Leek Mushroom Soup

**Time: 26 minutes**

**Serve: 4**

**Ingredients:**

- 5 cups mushrooms, chopped
- 4 cups vegetable stock
- 1 cup leek, chopped
- 1 tbsp olive oil
- Pepper
- Salt

**Directions:**

- Heat oil in a pan over medium heat.
- Add onion and leek and sauté until onion is softened. Transfer to the soup maker.
- Seal soup maker with lid and cook on smooth mode for 21 minutes.
- Season soup with salt and pepper.
- Serve and enjoy.

**Nutritional Value (Amount per Serving):**

- Calories 68
- Fat 3.9 g
- Carbohydrates 7 g
- Sugar 3.1 g
- Protein 3.5 g
- Cholesterol 0 mg

# 44-Cauliflower Broccoli Carrot Soup

**Time: 26 minutes**

**Serve: 4**

### Ingredients:

- 1 cup broccoli, chopped
- 1 cup carrot, chopped
- 2 cups cauliflower, chopped
- 2 vegetable stock cubes
- 4 cups of water
- Pepper
- Salt

### Directions:

- Add all ingredients into the soup maker and stir well.
- Seal soup maker with lid and cook on smooth mode for 21 minutes.
- Season soup with salt and pepper.
- Serve and enjoy.

## Nutritional Value (Amount per Serving):

- Calories 37
- Fat 0.3 g
- Carbohydrates 7.5 g
- Sugar 2.9 g
- Protein 2.1 g
- Cholesterol 0 mg

# 45-Roasted Eggplant Soup

**Time: 56 minutes**

**Serve: 4**

**Ingredients:**

- 2 large eggplants, sliced
- 1/2 tsp dried thyme
- 1/4 cup cilantro, chopped
- 1 tsp garlic, minced
- 1/4 cup parsley, chopped
- 14 oz can tomatoes, diced
- 4 cups vegetable stock
- 2 celery stalks, chopped
- 1 onion, chopped
- 1 tbsp olive oil
- 1/2 tsp cumin powder
- Pepper
- Salt

## Directions:

- Preheat the oven to 400 F/ 200 C.
- Place eggplants slices on a baking tray and sprinkle with cumin powder. Drizzle with oil.
- Roast eggplant in preheated oven for 25 minutes.
- Transfer roasted eggplant to the soup maker.
- Add remaining ingredients to the soup maker and stir well.
- Seal soup maker with lid and cook on smooth mode.
- Season soup with salt and pepper.
- Serve and enjoy.

## Nutritional Value (Amount per Serving):

- Calories 144
- Fat 9.8 g
- Carbohydrates 12.9 g
- Sugar 7.1 g
- Protein 2.8 g
- Cholesterol 8 mg

# 46-Flavorful Tomato Soup

**Time: 30 minutes**

**Serve: 4**

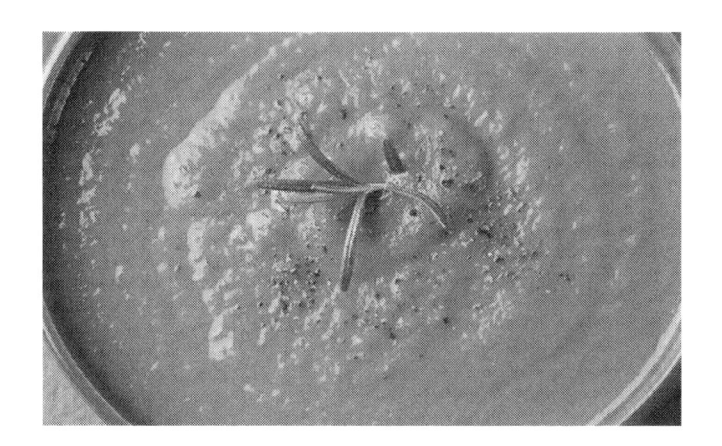

### Ingredients:

- 2 cups vegetable stock
- 1 tbsp brown sugar
- 28 oz can tomatoes, chopped
- 1 tsp garlic, crushed
- 1 medium onion, chopped
- 1 tbsp olive oil
- Pepper
- Salt

### Directions:

- Heat oil in a pan over medium heat.
- Add onion and sauté until onion is softened. Add garlic and sauté for 30 seconds.
- Transfer sautéed onion and garlic to the soup maker.

- Add remaining ingredients to the soup maker and stir well.
- Seal soup maker with lid and cook on smooth mode for 20 minutes.
- Season soup with salt and pepper.
- Serve and enjoy.

**Nutritional Value (Amount per Serving):**

- Calories 96
- Fat 3.6 g
- Carbohydrates 15.6 g
- Sugar 10.5 g
- Protein 2.3 g
- Cholesterol 0 mg

# 47-Creamy Tomato Soup

**Time: 35 minutes**

**Serve: 6**

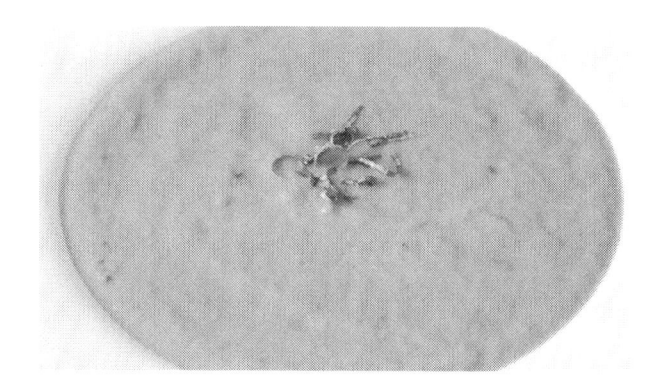

### Ingredients:

- 28 oz can tomatoes, chopped
- 3 cups vegetable stock
- 1 cup carrot, chopped
- 1 cup onion, chopped
- 2 tbsp butter,
- 1 1/2 tsp salt

### Directions:

- Melt butter in a pan over medium heat.
- Add onion, carrot, and 1/2 tsp salt and sauté for 5 minutes. Transfer to the soup maker.
- Add remaining ingredients to the soup maker and stir well.
- Seal soup maker with lid and cook on smooth mode for 25 minutes.
- Serve and enjoy.

## Nutritional Value (Amount per Serving):

- Calories 80
- Fat 3.9 g
- Carbohydrates 10.8 g
- Sugar 6.6 g
- Protein 1.8 g
- Cholesterol 10 mg

# 48-Bacon Tomato Soup

**Time: 30 minutes**

**Serve: 4**

**Ingredients:**

- 28 oz can tomatoes, crushed
- 2 1/2 cups chicken stock
- 2 tsp Italian seasoning
- 1 large carrot, chopped
- 2 celery stalks, chopped
- 1 tsp garlic, chopped
- 1 onion, chopped
- 2 bacon slices, cooked and chopped
- 1 tbsp olive oil
- Pepper
- Salt

## Directions:

- Heat oil in a pan over medium heat.
- Add onion, celery, and carrot and sauté for 5 minutes. Transfer to the soup maker.
- Add remaining ingredients to the soup maker and stir well.
- Seal soup maker with lid and cook on smooth mode for 21 minutes.
- Serve and enjoy.

## Nutritional Value (Amount per Serving):

- Calories 152
- Fat 7.9 g
- Carbohydrates 15.9 g
- Sugar 9.6 g
- Protein 6.3 g
- Cholesterol 11 mg

# 49-Parmesan Basil Tomato Soup

**Time: 30 minutes**

**Serve: 3**

## Ingredients:

- 14 oz can tomatoes, diced
- 2 tbsp fresh basil, chopped
- 1/2 cup parmesan cheese
- 1/2 cup heavy cream
- 2 cups chicken stock
- 2 tbsp flour
- 1/2 tsp dried oregano
- 1/2 tsp garlic, minced
- 1/2 cup carrot, diced
- 1/2 cup onion, diced
- 2 tbsp butter
- Pepper
- Salt

## Directions:

- Melt butter in a pan over medium heat.
- Add onion and sauté for 2 minutes. Add garlic and sauté for 30 seconds.
- Transfer onion and garlic to the soup maker.
- Add remaining ingredients to the soup maker and stir well.
- Seal soup maker with lid and cook on smooth mode for 21 minutes.
- Season soup with salt and pepper.
- Serve and enjoy.

## Nutritional Value (Amount per Serving):

- Calories 223
- Fat 16.6 g
- Carbohydrates 15.9 g
- Sugar 6.7 g
- Protein 4.7 g
- Cholesterol 51 mg

# 50-Creamy Squash Sweet Potato Soup

**Time: 30 minutes**

**Serve: 4**

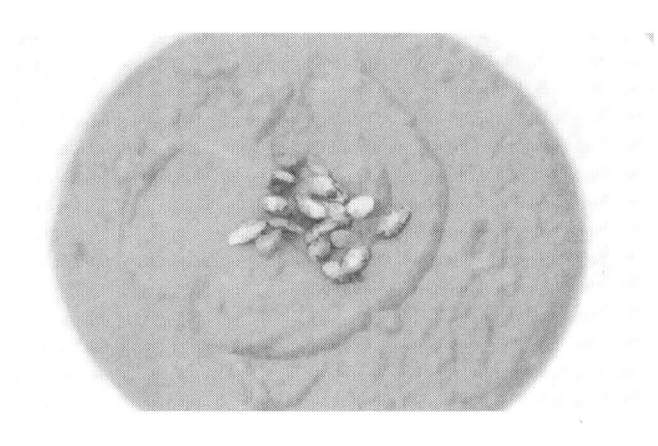

**Ingredients:**

- 3 1/2 cups butternut squash, diced
- 2 1/2 cups sweet potatoes, diced
- 1/2 tsp ground ginger
- 1/2 tsp allspice
- 1/2 tsp cumin powder
- 1/2 tsp ground coriander
- 1/2 tsp garlic, minced
- 2 cups of water
- 1 small onion, diced
- Pepper
- Salt

## Directions:

- Add all ingredients into the soup maker and stir well.
- Seal soup maker with lid and cook on smooth mode for 21 minutes.
- Season soup with salt and pepper.
- Serve and enjoy.

## Nutritional Value (Amount per Serving):

- Calories 175
- Fat 0.4 g
- Carbohydrates 42.5 g
- Sugar 3.9 g
- Protein 2.9 g
- Cholesterol 0 mg

# 51-Turkey Bean Soup

**Time: 40 minutes**

**Serve: 6**

**Ingredients:**

- 2 cups baby spinach, chopped
- 2 cups cooked turkey, shredded
- 14 oz can cannellini beans, rinsed and drained
- 2 cups of water
- 4 cups chicken stock
- 1/2 tsp cayenne pepper
- 1 1/2 tsp oregano
- 1 1/2 tsp dried parsley
- 1 jalapeno pepper, chopped
- 2 carrots, peeled and diced
- 1 leek, diced
- 1 onion, diced
- 1 tsp garlic, minced
- 2 tbsp olive oil
- Pepper
- Salt

## Directions:

- Heat oil in a pan over medium heat.
- Add carrots, jalapeno, leek, onion, and garlic and cook for 5-6 minutes. Transfer to the soup maker.
- Add remaining ingredients except turkey to the soup maker and stir well.
- Seal soup maker with lid and cook on chunky mode for 25 minutes.
- Add shredded turkey and stir well.
- Season soup with salt and pepper.
- Serve and enjoy.

## Nutritional Value (Amount per Serving):

- Calories 204
- Fat 7.6 g
- Carbohydrates 17.4 g
- Sugar 3 g
- Protein 18.8 g
- Cholesterol 35 mg

# 52-Chicken Mushroom Soup

**Time: 26 minutes**

**Serve: 4**

## Ingredients:

- 2 chicken breasts, boneless, cooked and shredded
- 1/2 tsp garlic, minced
- 1 tsp butter
- 4 mushrooms, chopped
- 1 onion, chopped
- 1 small carrot, chopped
- 2 cups of water
- 1 tsp cornflour
- 1 chicken stock cube
- Pepper
- Salt

## Directions:

- Add all ingredients into the soup maker and stir well.
- Seal soup maker with lid and cook on smooth mode for 21 minutes.
- Season soup with salt and pepper.
- Serve and enjoy.

## Nutritional Value (Amount per Serving):

- Calories 167
- Fat 6.3 g
- Carbohydrates 5.3 g
- Sugar 2.1 g
- Protein 21.5 g
- Cholesterol 65 mg

# 53-Creamy Mushroom Onion Soup

**Time: 30 minutes**

**Serve: 4**

**Ingredients:**

- 10 mushrooms, sliced
- 1 tbsp butter
- 2 tsp cornflour
- 1 chicken stock cube
- 1 tsp garlic, minced
- 1 potato, diced
- 2 small onion, diced
- Pepper
- Salt

**Directions:**

- Add all ingredients into the soup maker and stir everything well.
- Seal soup maker with lid and cook on smooth mode for 25 minutes.

- Season soup with salt and pepper.
- Serve and enjoy.

**Nutritional Value (Amount per Serving):**

- Calories 90
- Fat 3.2 g
- Carbohydrates 13.6 g
- Sugar 2.6 g
- Protein 3 g
- Cholesterol 8 mg

# 54-Thai Chicken Soup

**Time: 30 minutes**

**Serve: 4**

## Ingredients:

- 2 chicken breasts, boneless, cooked and shredded
- 1 tsp cornflour
- 1 potato, diced
- 1 onion, chopped
- 1 tbsp butter
- 1 tsp lemon juice
- 1 tsp Thai green curry paste
- 1 chicken stock cube
- 1 1/2 cups coconut milk
- 1/4 cup coriander, chopped
- 1/4 cup fresh basil, chopped
- 1 tsp garlic, minced
- 3 1/2 cups hot water
- Pepper
- Salt

## Directions:

- Add all ingredients into the soup maker and stir everything well.
- Seal soup maker with lid and cook on smooth mode for 25 minutes.
- Season soup with salt and pepper.
- Serve and enjoy.

## Nutritional Value (Amount per Serving):

- Calories 435
- Fat 31.3 g
- Carbohydrates 17.2 g
- Sugar 4.9 g
- Protein 24.1 g
- Cholesterol 70 mg

# 55-Chicken Sweet corn Soup

**Time: 30 minutes**

**Serve: 4**

## Ingredients:

- 2 chicken breasts, boneless, cooked, and shredded
- 1 tbsp butter
- 1 1/2 tbsp soy sauce
- 2 cups chicken stock
- 1 tsp cornflour
- 1/2 tsp ginger, grated
- 1 tsp garlic, minced
- 1/2 cup frozen sweet corn

## Directions:

- Add all ingredients into the soup maker and stir well.
- Seal soup maker with lid and cook on chunky mode for 25 minutes.
- Stir well and serve.

**Nutritional Value (Amount per Serving):**

- Calories 182
- Fat 8.6 g
- Carbohydrates 3.5 g
- Sugar 0.7 g
- Protein 21.5 g
- Cholesterol 70 mg

# 56-Thick & Creamy Pea Soup

**Time: 26 minutes**

**Serve: 4**

## Ingredients:

- 1 1/3 cup green split peas, rinsed and soaked overnight
- 3 cups vegetable stock
- 1 1/3 cup ham, cooked and shredded
- 1/2 tsp garlic, crushed
- 1 onion, chopped
- Pepper
- Salt

## Directions:

- Add all ingredients into the soup maker and stir well.
- Seal soup maker with lid and cook on chunky mode for 21 minutes.
- Season soup with salt and pepper.
- Serve and enjoy.

## Nutritional Value (Amount per Serving):

- Calories 313
- Fat 4.7 g
- Carbohydrates 44.8 g
- Sugar 7 g
- Protein 24.2 g
- Cholesterol 26 mg

# 57-Chili Squash Soup

**Time: 38 minutes**

**Serve: 4**

**Ingredients:**

- 1 lb butternut squash, diced
- 1 lime, juiced
- 1 cup of coconut milk
- 3 1/4 cups vegetable stock
- 1 tsp ginger, grated
- 1 red chili, sliced
- 1 tsp cumin powder
- 1 onion, chopped
- 2 tbsp olive oil
- Pepper
- Salt

**Directions:**

- Heat oil in a pan over medium heat.
- Add onion and sauté until softened. Transfer to the soup maker.

- Add remaining ingredients to the soup maker and stir well.
- Seal soup maker with lid and cook on chunky mode for 28 minutes.
- Season soup with salt and pepper.
- Serve and enjoy.

**Nutritional Value (Amount per Serving):**

- Calories 272
- Fat 21.7 g
- Carbohydrates 21.5 g
- Sugar 6.5 g
- Protein 3.3 g
- Cholesterol 0 mg

# 58-Delicious Asian Chicken Soup

**Time: 26 minutes**

**Serve: 4**

**Ingredients:**

- 2 chicken breasts, cooked and diced
- 4 cups chicken stock
- 1/2 cup spring onions, sliced
- 2 tbsp ginger, grated
- 1 tsp garlic, crushed
- 1 1/2 red chili, sliced
- 1 dried lemongrass
- 1 tbsp lemon juice
- 3 tbsp Thai curry paste

**Directions:**

- Add all ingredients into the soup maker and stir well.
- Seal soup maker with lid and cook on smooth mode for 21 minutes.
- Stir well and serve.

**Nutritional Value (Amount per Serving):**

- Calories 171
- Fat 6 g
- Carbohydrates 6.6 g
- Sugar 2 g
- Protein 21.5 g
- Cholesterol 62 mg

# 59-Root Vegetable Soup

**Time: 30 minutes**

**Serve: 4**

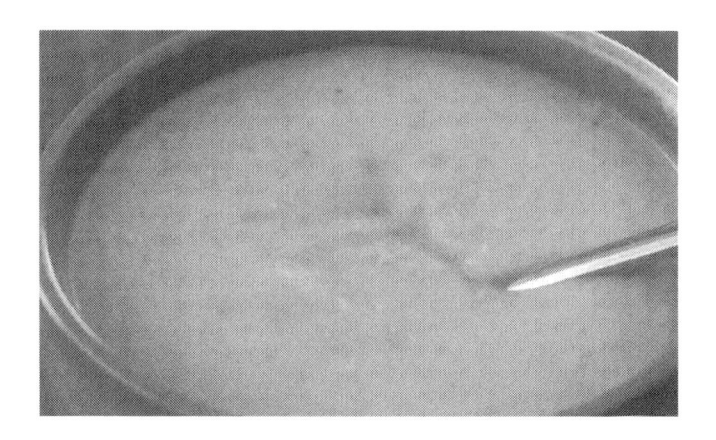

### Ingredients:

- 1 lb Swede, peeled and chopped
- 1/4 lb parsnips, peeled and chopped
- 1/2 lb carrots, peeled and chopped
- 1 tsp garlic, crushed
- 1 small onion, chopped
- 1 tbsp olive oil
- 1 tsp allspice
- 2 3/4 cups vegetable stock
- Pepper
- Salt

### Directions:

- Heat oil in a pan over medium heat.
- Add garlic and onion and sauté for 2 minutes. Transfer to the soup maker.

- Add remaining ingredients to the soup maker and stir well.
- Seal soup maker with lid and cook on smooth mode for 21 minutes.
- Season soup with salt and pepper.
- Serve and enjoy.

**Nutritional Value (Amount per Serving):**

- Calories 129
- Fat 4 g
- Carbohydrates 22.8 g
- Sugar 11.7 g
- Protein 2.7 g
- Cholesterol 0 mg

# 60-Simple Courgette Leek Soup

**Time: 30 minutes**

**Serve: 4**

**Ingredients:**

- 2 courgettes, chopped
- 2 tbsp olive oil
- 3 cups vegetable stock
- 1 potato, diced
- 2 celery sticks, chopped
- 3 leeks, chopped
- Pepper
- Salt

**Directions:**

- Heat oil in a pan over medium heat.
- Add courgettes, potato, celery, and leeks and cook for 5 minutes. Transfer to the soup maker.
- Add remaining ingredients to the soup maker and stir well.

- Seal soup maker with lid and cook on smooth mode for 21 minutes.
- Season soup with salt and pepper.
- Serve and enjoy.

**Nutritional Value (Amount per Serving):**

- Calories 157
- Fat 7.5 g
- Carbohydrates 21.4 g
- Sugar 5.4 g
- Protein 3.5 g
- Cholesterol 0 mg

# 61-Vegan Potato Soup

**Time: 30 minutes**

**Serve: 4**

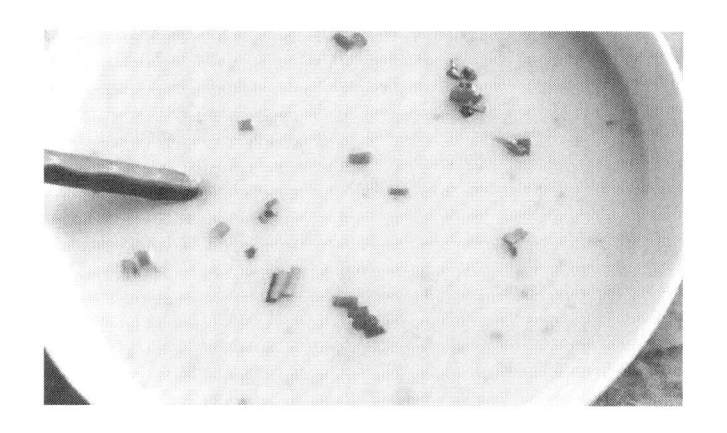

**Ingredients:**

- 4 medium potatoes, peeled and diced
- 14 oz coconut milk
- 4 cups vegetable stock
- 2 carrots, chopped
- 1/2 tsp dried rosemary
- 1/2 tsp dried thyme
- 1 tbsp olive oil
- 1 tsp garlic, crushed
- 1 onion, chopped
- Pepper
- Salt

## Directions:

- Heat oil in a pan over medium heat.
- Add onion and garlic and sauté until onion is softened. Transfer to the soup maker.
- Add remaining ingredients to the soup maker and stir well.
- Seal soup maker with lid and cook on smooth mode for 21 minutes.
- Season soup with salt and pepper.
- Serve and enjoy.

## Nutritional Value (Amount per Serving):

- Calories 437
- Fat 27.5 g
- Carbohydrates 45.9 g
- Sugar 9.1 g
- Protein 6.9 g
- Cholesterol 0 mg

# 62-Creamy Leek Potato Soup

**Time: 30 minutes**

**Serve: 4**

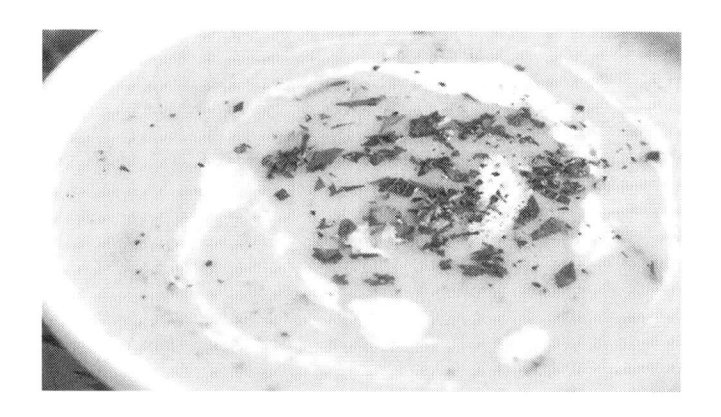

**Ingredients:**

- 4 potatoes, peeled and chopped
- 3 leeks, chopped
- 1/4 cup fresh parsley, chopped
- 1/2 tsp dried thyme
- 1/8 tsp dried marjoram
- 4 cups chicken stock
- 2 tbsp butter
- 1 tsp salt

**Directions:**

- Melt butter in a pan over medium heat.
- Add leek and saute until softened. Transfer to the soup maker.
- Add remaining ingredients to the soup maker and stir well.

- Seal soup maker with lid and cook on smooth mode for 21 minutes.
- Serve and enjoy.

**Nutritional Value (Amount per Serving):**

- Calories 250
- Fat 6.8 g
- Carbohydrates 44 g
- Sugar 5.8 g
- Protein 5.4 g
- Cholesterol 15 mg

# 63-Tomato Cabbage Soup

**Time: 35 minutes**

**Serve: 4**

**Ingredients:**

- 7 oz can tomatoes, chopped
- 1/4 cabbage head, chopped
- 1 celery stalk, chopped
- 2 carrots, peeled and chopped
- 1/4 tsp dried thyme
- 4 cups chicken stock
- 1 garlic clove, minced
- 1 small onion, chopped
- 1 tbsp olive oil
- Pepper
- Salt

## Directions:

- Heat oil in a pan over medium heat.
- Add onion and garlic and sauté for 2-3 minutes. Transfer to the soup maker.
- Add remaining ingredients to the soup maker and stir well.
- Seal soup maker with lid and cook on chunky mode for 25 minutes.
- Season soup with salt and pepper.
- Serve and enjoy.

## Nutritional Value (Amount per Serving):

- Calories 83
- Fat 4.1 g
- Carbohydrates 10.9 g
- Sugar 6.1 g
- Protein 2.2 g
- Cholesterol 0 mg

# 64-Zucchini Coconut Soup

**Time: 30 minutes**

**Serve: 4**

## Ingredients:

- 1 lb zucchini, sliced
- 1/2 cup coconut milk
- 3 cups vegetable stock
- 1 tsp garlic, minced
- 1/2 onion, chopped
- 1 tbsp olive oil
- Pepper
- Salt

## Directions:

- Heat oil in a pan over medium heat.
- Add onion and garlic and sauté until onion is softened. Transfer to the soup maker.
- Add remaining ingredients to the soup maker and stir well.

- Seal soup maker with lid and cook on smooth mode for 21 minutes.
- Season soup with salt and pepper.
- Serve and enjoy.

**Nutritional Value (Amount per Serving):**

- Calories 128
- Fat 10.9 g
- Carbohydrates 7.7 g
- Sugar 4.1 g
- Protein 2.6 g
- Cholesterol 0 mg

# 65-Cheesy Spinach Soup

**Time: 20 minutes**

**Serve: 3**

**Ingredients:**

- 10 oz fresh spinach, chopped
- 2 tbsp butter
- 1 onion, chopped
- 1/2 tsp garlic, minced
- 1 cup cream cheese
- 2 cups of water
- Pepper
- Salt

**Directions:**

- Melt butter in a pan over medium heat.
- Add onion and garlic and sauté until onion is softened. Transfer to the soup maker.
- Add remaining ingredients except cream cheese to the soup maker and stir well.

- Seal soup maker with lid and cook on smooth mode for 10 minutes.
- Add cream cheese and stir well.
- Season soup with salt and pepper.
- Serve and enjoy.

**Nutritional Value (Amount per Serving):**

- Calories 375
- Fat 35.1 g
- Carbohydrates 9.1 g
- Sugar 2.1 g
- Protein 9.1 g
- Cholesterol 105 mg

## 66-Healthy Spinach Soup

**Time: 25 minutes**

**Serve: 4**

**Ingredients:**

- 1 lb spinach, chopped
- 1 potato, peeled and chopped
- 1/2 cup heavy cream
- 4 cups vegetable stock
- 1/2 tsp garlic, minced
- 1/4 cup green onion, chopped
- 1 onion, chopped
- 2 tbsp olive oil
- Pepper
- Salt

**Directions:**

- Heat oil in a pan over medium heat.
- Add onion, garlic, and green onion and sauté until onion is softened. Transfer to the soup maker.

- Add remaining ingredients except for heavy cream to the soup maker and stir well.
- Seal soup maker with lid and cook on smooth mode for 15 minutes.
- Add heavy cream and stir well.
- Season soup with salt and pepper.
- Serve and enjoy.

**Nutritional Value (Amount per Serving):**

- Calories 190
- Fat 13.2 g
- Carbohydrates 16 g
- Sugar 2.9 g
- Protein 5.2 g
- Cholesterol 21 mg

# 67-Easy Mint Pea Soup

**Time: 30 minutes**

**Serve: 4**

## Ingredients:

- 4 1/3 cups frozen peas
- 4 cups vegetable stock
- 2 tbsp fresh mint leaves
- 1 onion, chopped
- Pepper
- Salt

## Directions:

- Add all ingredients to the soup maker and stir well.
- Seal soup maker with lid and cook on smooth mode for 25 minutes.
- Season soup with salt and pepper.
- Serve and enjoy.

**Nutritional Value (Amount per Serving):**

- Calories 154
- Fat 0.6 g
- Carbohydrates 28.5 g
- Sugar 9.9 g
- Protein 9.7 g
- Cholesterol 0 mg

# 68-Pea Bacon Soup

**Time: 30 minutes**

**Serve: 4**

## Ingredients:

- 3 cups fresh peas
- 1 lemon juice
- 2 tbsp fresh thyme
- 4 cups chicken stock
- ½ tsp garlic, chopped
- 2 medium leeks, sliced
- 3 bacon slices, cooked and chopped
- 1 tbsp olive oil
- Pepper
- Salt

## Directions:

- Heat oil in a pan over medium heat.
- Add onion and garlic and sauté for 3-4 minutes.
- Transfer sautéed onion and garlic to the soup maker.

- Add remaining ingredients except for bacon and stir well.
- Seal soup maker with lid and cook on smooth mode for 21 minutes.
- Add bacon and stir well. Season soup with salt and pepper.
- Serve and enjoy.

**Nutritional Value (Amount per Serving):**

- Calories 239
- Fat 10.8 g
- Carbohydrates 24.2 g
- Sugar 8.9 g
- Protein 12.8 g
- Cholesterol 16 mg

# 69-Easy Broccoli Soup

**Time: 30 minutes**

**Serve: 3**

**Ingredients:**

- 4 cups broccoli, chopped
- 2 ½ cups chicken stock
- 1 small shallot, minced
- ½ tsp garlic, minced
- 1 tbsp butter
- Pepper
- Salt

**Directions:**

- Melt butter in a pan over medium heat.
- Add shallot and garlic sauté until shallot is softened. Transfer to the soup maker.
- Add remaining ingredients to the soup maker and stir well.

- Seal soup maker with lid and cook on smooth mode for 15 minutes.
- Season soup with salt and pepper.
- Serve and enjoy.

**Nutritional Value (Amount per Serving):**

- Calories 87
- Fat 4.7 g
- Carbohydrates 9.4 g
- Sugar 2.7 g
- Protein 4.1 g
- Cholesterol 10 mg

# 70-Parmesan Asparagus Soup

**Time: 35 minutes**

**Serve: 4**

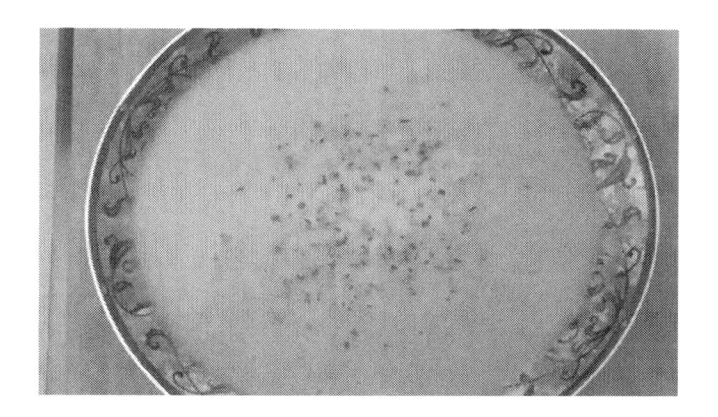

**Ingredients:**

- 1 ½ lbs asparagus, trimmed and chopped
- ½ cup parmesan cheese, grated
- ½ tsp dried thyme
- 4 cups vegetable stock
- ½ tsp garlic, crushed
- 1 onion, chopped
- 1 tbsp lemon juice
- 1 tbsp butter
- Pepper
- Salt

**Directions:**

- Melt butter in a pan over medium heat.
- Add onion and garlic and sauté until onion is softened.
- Transfer sautéed onion and garlic to the soup maker.

- Add remaining ingredients except cheese and lemon juice to the soup maker and stir well.
- Seal soup maker with lid and cook on smooth mode for 21 minutes.
- Add cheese and lemon juice and stir well. Season soup with salt and pepper.
- Serve and enjoy.

**Nutritional Value (Amount per Serving):**

- Calories 90
- Fat 4 g
- Carbohydrates 10.5 g
- Sugar 5.2 g
- Protein 5.7 g
- Cholesterol 10 mg

# 71-Cashew Asparagus Soup

**Time: 20 minutes**

**Serve: 4**

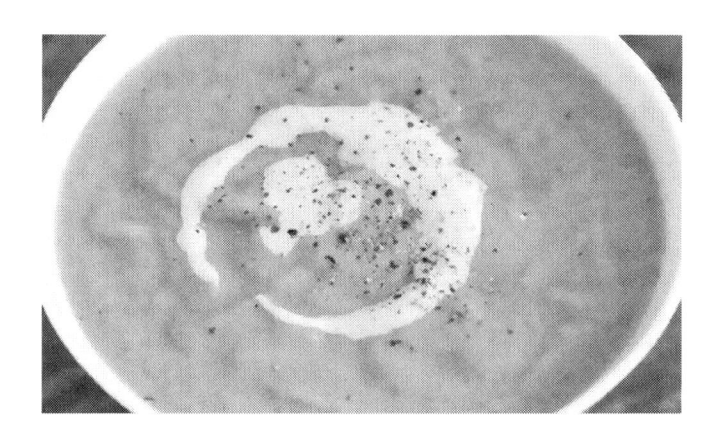

## Ingredients:

- 1 ½ lbs asparagus, chopped
- 1 cup cashews, soaked for 2 hours
- 1 ½ cups vegetable stock
- Pepper
- Salt

## Directions:

- Add all ingredients to the soup maker and stir well.
- Seal soup maker with lid and cook on smooth mode for 10 minutes.
- Season soup with salt and pepper.
- Serve and enjoy.

**Nutritional Value (Amount per Serving):**

- Calories 233
- Fat 16.1 g
- Carbohydrates 18.2 g
- Sugar 5.2 g
- Protein 9.1 g
- Cholesterol 0 mg

## 72-Vegan Celery Soup

**Time: 26 minutes**

**Serve: 4**

**Ingredients:**

- 6 cups celery, chopped
- 2 cups vegetable stock
- ½ tsp dill
- 1 cup of coconut milk
- 1 onion, chopped
- 1 tbsp olive oil
- Pepper
- Salt

**Directions:**

- Heat oil in a pan over medium heat.
- Add onion and sauté until softened. Transfer to the soup maker.
- Add remaining ingredients to the soup maker and stir well.

- Seal soup maker with lid and cook on smooth mode for 21 minutes.
- Season soup with salt and pepper.
- Serve and enjoy.

**Nutritional Value (Amount per Serving):**

- Calories 207
- Fat 18.2 g
- Carbohydrates 10.9 g
- Sugar 5.6 g
- Protein 3 g
- Cholesterol 0 mg

# 73-Brussels Sprouts Cauliflower Soup

**Time: 30 minutes**

**Serve: 6**

**Ingredients:**

- 1 small cauliflower head, chopped
- 1 lb Brussels sprouts
- 1 tsp garlic, crushed
- 1 tbsp olive oil
- 1 onion, chopped
- ½ cup coconut cream
- 4 cups vegetable stock
- Pepper
- Salt

**Directions:**

- Heat oil in a pan over medium heat.
- Add onion and garlic and sauté for 2-3 minutes. Transfer to the soup maker.

- Add remaining ingredients except for coconut cream to the soup maker and stir well.
- Seal soup maker with lid and cook on smooth mode for 21 minutes.
- Add coconut cream and stir well. Season soup with salt and pepper.
- Serve and enjoy.

**Nutritional Value (Amount per Serving):**

- Calories 115
- Fat 7.5 g
- Carbohydrates 13.3 g
- Sugar 4 g
- Protein 3.9 g
- Cholesterol 0 mg

# 74-Creamy Carrot Sprout Soup

**Time:** 30 minutes

**Serve:** 4

## Ingredients:

- 2 medium carrots, chopped
- 1 lb Brussels sprouts, chopped
- 2 tbsp fresh parsley, chopped
- 3 cups vegetable stock
- 1 celery stalk, chopped
- 1 onion, chopped
- 2 tbsp olive oil
- Pepper
- Salt

## Directions:

- Heat oil in a pan over medium heat.
- Add onion and sauté until onion is softened. Transfer to the soup maker.

- Add remaining ingredients to the soup maker and stir well.
- Seal soup maker with lid and cook on smooth mode for 21 minutes.
- Season soup with salt and pepper.
- Serve and enjoy.

**Nutritional Value (Amount per Serving):**

- Calories 138
- Fat 7.5 g
- Carbohydrates 16.8 g
- Sugar 5.7 g
- Protein 4.8 g
- Cholesterol 0 mg

# 75-Cinnamon Squash Apple Soup

**Time: 26 minutes**

**Serve: 6**

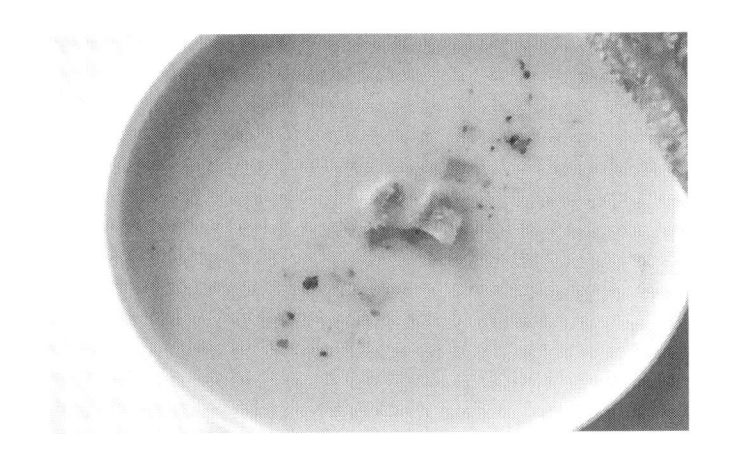

**Ingredients:**

- 1 cup apple, chopped
- 3 cups butternut squash, chopped
- 1/8 tsp nutmeg
- ½ tsp cinnamon
- 1 bell pepper, chopped
- 1 onion, chopped
- 5 cups vegetable stock
- Pepper
- Salt

**Directions:**

- Add all ingredients into the soup maker and stir well.
- Seal soup maker with lid and cook on smooth mode for 21 minutes.

- Season soup with salt and pepper.
- Serve and enjoy.

**Nutritional Value (Amount per Serving):**

- Calories 70
- Fat 0.3 g
- Carbohydrates 17.5 g
- Sugar 7.8 g
- Protein 1.5 g
- Cholesterol 0 mg

# 76-Bean Veggie Minestrone Soup

**Time: 38 minutes**

**Serve: 4**

### Ingredients:

- 1 1/2 cups mixed vegetables, chopped
- 2 tbsp Italian seasoning
- 14 oz can kidney beans, rinsed and drained
- 28 oz can tomatoes, crushed
- 15 oz chicken stock

### Directions:

- Add all ingredients into the soup maker and stir well.
- Seal soup maker with lid and cook on chunky mode for 28 minutes.
- Serve and enjoy.

**Nutritional Value (Amount per Serving):**

- Calories 204
- Fat 2.4 g
- Carbohydrates 36.2 g
- Sugar 10.6 g
- Protein 10.2 g
- Cholesterol 5 mg

# 77-Blue Cheese Brussels Sprout Soup

**Time: 30 minutes**

**Serve: 4**

**Ingredients:**

- 1 lb Brussels sprouts, chopped
- 1 tbsp butter
- 1/4 cup blue cheese, crumbled
- 4 cups vegetable stock
- 1 leek, chopped

**Directions:**

- Melt butter in a pan over medium heat.
- Add leek and sprouts and sauté for 5 minutes. Transfer to the soup maker.
- Add stock to the soup maker and stir well.
- Seal soup maker with lid and cook on smooth mode for 21 minutes.
- Top with crumbled cheese and serve.

**Nutritional Value (Amount per Serving):**

- Calories 124
- Fat 5.9 g
- Carbohydrates 14.6 g
- Sugar 4.1 g
- Protein 6.4 g
- Cholesterol 14 mg

# 78-Caprese Soup

**Time: 20 minutes**

**Serve: 4**

**Ingredients:**

- 12 basil leaves, chopped
- 2 cups chicken stock
- 4 cups roasted tomatoes
- Pepper
- Salt

**Directions:**

- Add all ingredients into the soup maker and stir well.
- Seal soup maker with lid and cook on smooth mode for 15 minutes.
- Season soup with salt and pepper.
- Serve and enjoy.

**Nutritional Value (Amount per Serving):**

- Calories 445
- Fat 34.3 g
- Carbohydrates 44.4 g
- Sugar 0.4 g
- Protein 0.4 g
- Cholesterol 0 mg

# 79-Healthy & Easy Tomato Soup

**Time: 20 minutes**

**Serve: 6**

**Ingredients:**

- 28 oz can tomatoes, crushed
- 1/2 cup carrot juice
- 5 garlic cloves, crushed
- Pepper
- Salt

**Directions:**

- Add all ingredients into the soup maker and stir well.
- Seal soup maker with lid and cook on smooth mode for 15 minutes.
- Season soup with salt and pepper.
- Serve and enjoy.

**Nutritional Value (Amount per Serving):**

- Calories 36
- Fat 0 g
- Carbohydrates 8.5 g
- Sugar 5 g
- Protein 1.4 g
- Cholesterol 0 mg

# 80-Vegan Kale Miso Soup

**Time: 15 minutes**

**Serve: 2**

## Ingredients:

- 1/2 cup kale, chopped
- 1/2 cup green onions, chopped
- 1/2 tsp garlic, minced
- 2 tbsp light yellow miso
- 4 cups of water

## Directions:

- In a small bowl, whisk together miso and warm water until smooth consistency.
- Add all ingredients into the soup maker and stir well.
- Seal soup maker with lid and cook on smooth mode for 10 minutes.
- Serve and enjoy.

**Nutritional Value (Amount per Serving):**

- Calories 47
- Fat 0.1 g
- Carbohydrates 6.8 g
- Sugar 3.6 g
- Protein 4 g
- Cholesterol 0 mg

# 81-Creamy Potato Soup

**Time: 30 minutes**

**Serve: 4**

**Ingredients:**

- 3 1/2 cup mashed potatoes
- 1/4 cup milk
- 14.5 oz chicken stock
- 1/2 onion, chopped
- 1 tbsp butter

**Directions:**

- Melt butter in a pan over medium heat.
- Add onion and sauté for 2 minutes. Transfer to the soup maker.
- Add remaining ingredients to the soup maker and stir everything well.
- Seal soup maker with lid and cook on smooth mode for 21 minutes.
- Serve and enjoy.

**Nutritional Value (Amount per Serving):**

- Calories 219
- Fat 6 g
- Carbohydrates 36.5 g
- Sugar 1.6 g
- Protein 5.9 g
- Cholesterol 13 mg

# 82-Broccoli Lemon Soup

**Time: 33 minutes**

**Serve: 4**

## Ingredients:

- 1 1/2 lbs broccoli, chopped
- 1 tbsp fresh lemon juice
- 1 cup almond milk
- 2 cups of water
- 1/4 cup parmesan cheese, grated

## Directions:

- Add broccoli, almond milk, water, and half cheese to the soup maker and stir well.
- Seal soup maker with lid and cook on chunky mode for 28 minutes.
- Add lemon juice and remaining cheese and stir well.
- Serve and enjoy.

## Nutritional Value (Amount per Serving):

- Calories 202
- Fat 15.3 g
- Carbohydrates 14.8 g
- Sugar 5 g
- Protein 6.7 g
- Cholesterol 1 mg

# 83-Versatile Vegetable Soup

**Time: 25 minutes**

**Serve: 3**

**Ingredients:**

- 2/3 cup celery, chopped
- 2/3 cup carrots, chopped
- 1 1/2 cups potato, chopped
- 1 onion, chopped
- 1 tbsp olive oil
- 2 1/2 cups vegetable stock
- 1 tsp dried mixed herbs
- Pepper
- Salt

**Directions:**

- Heat oil in a pan over medium heat.
- Add onion and sauté until softened. Transfer to the soup maker.
- Add remaining ingredients to the soup maker and stir well.

- Seal soup maker with lid and cook on smooth mode for 15 minutes.
- Season soup with salt and pepper.
- Serve and enjoy.

**Nutritional Value (Amount per Serving):**

- Calories 103
- Fat 4.9 g
- Carbohydrates 14 g
- Sugar 3.9 g
- Protein 1.9 g
- Cholesterol 0 mg

# 84-Lime Sweet Corn Soup

**Time: 38 minutes**

**Serve: 6**

## Ingredients:

- 5 cups fresh sweet corn
- 2 lime juice
- 2 tbsp parsley
- 4 cups chicken stock
- 1 garlic, minced
- 1 small onion, chopped
- 1 small carrot, chopped
- 1 small potato, chopped
- 1 tbsp olive oil
- Pepper
- Salt

**Directions:**

- Heat oil in a pan over medium heat.
- Add onion and garlic and sauté for 2-3 minutes. Transfer to the soup maker.
- Add remaining ingredients to the soup maker and cook on chunky mode for 28 minutes.
- Season soup with salt and pepper.
- Serve and enjoy.

**Nutritional Value (Amount per Serving):**

- Calories 173
- Fat 4.3 g
- Carbohydrates 33.3 g
- Sugar 6 g
- Protein 5.6 g
- Cholesterol 0 mg

# 85-Corn Veg Soup

**Time: 25 minutes**

**Serve: 3**

**Ingredients:**

- 1/2 cup sweet corn
- 1 tbsp spring onion, chopped
- 1 tbsp green beans, chopped
- 1 tbsp carrot, chopped
- 1 tbsp butter
- 2 tbsp cornflour
- 3 cups of water
- Pepper
- Salt

**Directions:**

- Melt butter in a pan over medium heat.
- Add corn, spring onion, green beans, and carrot and sauté for 2 minutes. Transfer to the soup maker.

- In a small bowl, whisk together cornflour and 2 tbsp water and pour it into the soup maker.
- Add water, pepper, and salt to the soup maker and stir well.
- Seal soup maker with lid and cook on chunky mode for 15 minutes.
- Serve and enjoy.

**Nutritional Value (Amount per Serving):**

- Calories 76
- Fat 4.3 g
- Carbohydrates 91 g
- Sugar 1.1 g
- Protein 1.3 g
- Cholesterol 10 mg

# 86-Mexican Corn Soup

**Time: 38 minutes**

**Serve: 4**

**Ingredients:**

- 14 oz cream of corn
- 2 tbsp olive oil
- 2 1/2 cups vegetable stock
- 3 tbsp salsa
- 1 1/2 tsp vinegar
- 1 green chili, chopped
- 1 tsp garlic, chopped
- 1 small onion, chopped
- 2 tbsp tomato puree
- 1 tsp red chili flakes
- 1 tsp dried cilantro
- 1/2 tsp cumin powder
- Salt

## Directions:

- Heat oil in a pan over medium heat.
- Add onion, green chili, and garlic and sauté for 2 minutes. Transfer to the soup maker.
- Add remaining ingredients to the soup maker and stir well.
- Seal soup maker with lid and cook on chunky mode for 28 minutes.
- Serve and enjoy.

## Nutritional Value (Amount per Serving):

- Calories 170
- Fat 14.8 g
- Carbohydrates 8.1 g
- Sugar 4 g
- Protein 2.4 g
- Cholesterol 0 mg

# 87-Garlic Corn Soup

**Time: 30 minutes**

**Serve: 4**

**Ingredients:**

- 4 cups corn
- 1 tbsp olive oil
- 6 cups vegetable stock
- 1 shallot, chopped
- 6 garlic cloves, chopped
- Pepper
- Salt

**Directions:**

- Heat oil in a pan over medium heat.
- Add shallot and garlic and sauté for 2-3 minutes. Transfer to the soup maker.
- Add remaining ingredients to the soup maker and stir well.

- Seal soup maker with lid and cook on smooth mode for 21 minutes.
- Season soup with salt and pepper.
- Serve and enjoy.

**Nutritional Value (Amount per Serving):**

- Calories 180
- Fat 5.5 g
- Carbohydrates 32.3 g
- Sugar 6.1 g
- Protein 6 g
- Cholesterol 0 mg

# 88-Apple Pumpkin Soup

**Time: 30 minutes**

**Serve: 4**

### Ingredients:

- 1 cup green apple, chopped
- 2 cups pumpkin, cubed
- 1 onion, chopped
- 1 tsp garlic, chopped
- 2 tbsp olive oil
- 2 cups vegetable stock
- Pepper
- Salt

### Directions:

- Heat oil in a pan over medium heat.
- Add onion and garlic and sauté for 2-3 minutes. Transfer to the soup maker.
- Add remaining ingredients to the soup maker and stir well.

- Seal soup maker with lid and cook on smooth mode for 20 minutes.
- Season soup with salt and pepper.
- Serve and enjoy.

**Nutritional Value (Amount per Serving):**

- Calories 146
- Fat 7.5 g
- Carbohydrates 20.9 g
- Sugar 11.4 g
- Protein 2 g
- Cholesterol 0 mg

# 89-Apple Ginger Squash Soup

**Time: 30 minutes**

**Serve: 6**

**Ingredients:**

- 2 cups carrots, chopped
- 5 cups vegetable stock
- 1 1/2 cups unsweetened applesauce
- 1/4 tsp cinnamon
- 1 tsp curry powder
- 1/2 tsp turmeric
- 1/2 tsp garlic, minced
- 1 tbsp ginger, grated
- 2 cups butternut squash, cubed
- 1 onion, chopped
- 1 tbsp olive oil
- Salt

## Directions:

- Heat oil in a pan over medium heat.
- Add onion and garlic and sauté until onion is softened. Transfer to the soup maker.
- Add remaining ingredients to the soup maker and stir well.
- Seal soup maker with lid and cook on smooth mode for 21 minutes.
- Serve and enjoy.

## Nutritional Value (Amount per Serving):

- Calories 100
- Fat 2.6 g
- Carbohydrates 19.5 g
- Sugar 10.4 g
- Protein 1.5 g
- Cholesterol 0 mg

# 90-Apple Parsnip Soup

**Time: 35 minutes**

**Serve: 6**

**Ingredients:**

- 3 apples, peeled, cored, and chopped
- 1/2 cup heavy cream
- 4 cups vegetable stock
- 1 tbsp fresh thyme, chopped
- 1 lb parsnips, peeled and chopped
- 1 tsp garlic, minced
- 1 onion, chopped
- 1 tbsp olive oil
- Pepper
- Salt

**Directions:**

- Heat oil in a pan over medium heat.
- Add onion and garlic and sauté until onion is softened. Transfer to the soup maker.

- Add remaining ingredients except for cream to the soup maker and stir well.
- Seal soup maker with lid and cook on smooth mode for 21 minutes.
- Add heavy cream and stir well. Season with salt and pepper.
- Serve and enjoy.

**Nutritional Value (Amount per Serving):**

- Calories 183
- Fat 6.6 g
- Carbohydrates 32.1 g
- Sugar 16.5 g
- Protein 2 g
- Cholesterol 14 mg

# 91-Pear Parsnip Soup

**Time: 30 minutes**

**Serve: 4**

### Ingredients:

- 1 cup pears, peeled and chopped
- 1/2 cup heavy cream
- 5 cups vegetable stock
- 1 cup dry white wine
- 1/2 cup celery, chopped
- 2 cups parsnips, peeled and chopped
- 1/4 cup onion, chopped
- 2 tbsp butter
- Pepper
- Salt

### Directions:

- Melt butter in a pan over medium heat.
- Add onion and celery and sauté until onion is softened. Transfer to the soup maker.

- Add remaining ingredients except for heavy cream to the soup maker and stir well.
- Seal soup maker with lid and cook on smooth mode for 21 minutes.
- Add heavy cream and stir well.
- Season with salt and pepper.
- Serve and enjoy.

**Nutritional Value (Amount per Serving):**

- Calories 237
- Fat 11.7 g
- Carbohydrates 22.3 g
- Sugar 9 g
- Protein 2 g
- Cholesterol 36 mg

# 92-Squash Pear Soup

**Time: 30 minutes**

**Serve: 4**

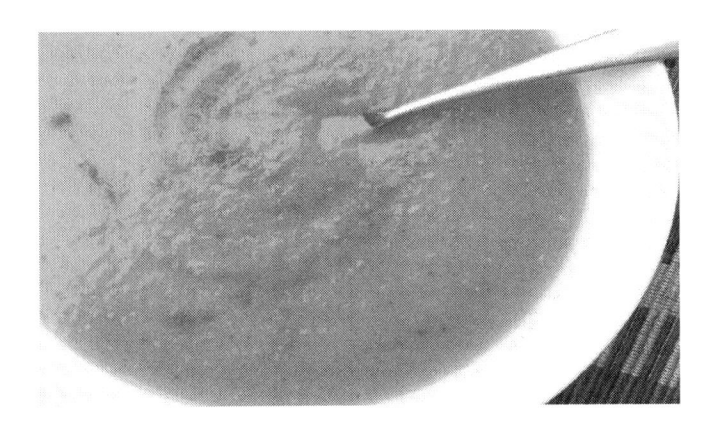

**Ingredients:**

- 2 lbs butternut squash, roasted and chopped
- 1 tbsp vinegar
- 3 cups vegetable stock
- 1 1/2 tsp dried sage
- 2 pears, peeled and chopped
- 2 celery, peeled and chopped
- 2 carrots, peeled and chopped
- 1 tsp garlic, minced
- 1 onion, chopped
- 2 tbsp olive oil
- Pepper
- Salt

**Directions:**

- Heat oil in a pan over medium heat.
- Add onion and garlic and sauté for 2-3 minutes. Transfer to the soup maker.
- Add remaining ingredients to the soup maker and stir well.
- Seal soup maker with lid and cook on smooth mode for 21 minutes.
- Season soup with salt and pepper.
- Serve and enjoy.

**Nutritional Value (Amount per Serving):**

- Calories 256
- Fat 7.6 g
- Carbohydrates 49.7 g
- Sugar 18.7 g
- Protein 3.7 g
- Cholesterol 0 mg

# 93-Celery Pear Soup

**Time: 30 minutes**

**Serve: 4**

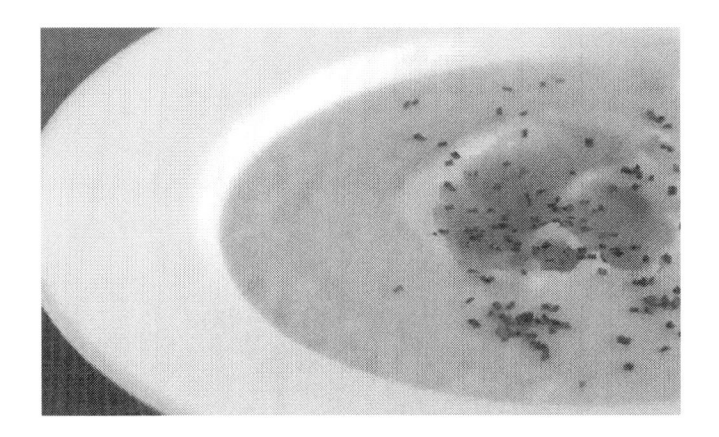

**Ingredients:**

- 1 1/4 cups celery stalks, chopped
- 1 tbsp fresh lemon juice
- 3 1/4 cups vegetable stock
- 1 1/2 cups pears, chopped
- 1 onion, chopped
- 3 cups celery root, cubed
- 2 tbsp olive oil

**Directions:**

- Heat oil in a pan over medium heat.
- Add onion, celery stalks, and celery root and saute until onion is softened. Transfer to the soup maker.
- Add remaining ingredients except lemon juice to the soup maker and stir well.

- Seal soup maker with lid and cook on smooth mode for 21 minutes.
- Add lemon juice and stir well. Season soup with salt and pepper.
- Serve and enjoy.

**Nutritional Value (Amount per Serving):**

- Calories 166
- Fat 7.6 g
- Carbohydrates 24.3 g
- Sugar 10 g
- Protein 2.9 g
- Cholesterol 0 mg

# 94-Artichoke Tomato Soup

**Time: 30 minutes**

**Serve: 4**

## Ingredients:

- 28 oz can tomatoes, diced
- 4 cups chicken stock
- 14 oz can artichoke hearts, drained and chopped
- 1/2 tsp garlic, minced
- 1 tsp dried basil
- 1/2 tsp dried thyme
- 1 onion, chopped
- 2 tbsp olive oil
- 1/2 cup sour cream
- Pepper
- Salt

## Directions:

- Heat oil in a pan over medium heat.
- Add onion and garlic and sauté until onion is softened. Transfer to the soup maker.
- Add remaining ingredients except for sour cream to the soup maker and stir well.
- Seal soup maker with lid and cook on smooth mode for 21 minutes.
- Add sour cream and stir well. Season soup with salt and pepper.
- Serve and enjoy.

## Nutritional Value (Amount per Serving):

- Calories 215
- Fat 13.6 g
- Carbohydrates 19.8 g
- Sugar 9.5 g
- Protein 5.4 g
- Cholesterol 13 mg

# 95-Herb Tomato Artichoke Soup

**Time: 20 minutes**

**Serve: 4**

### Ingredients:

- 28 oz can tomatoes, diced
- 1 cup milk
- 1 tsp basil
- 1/2 tsp oregano
- 1 1/2 cups water
- 14 oz can artichokes, chopped
- 2 tbsp butter
- 1 garlic clove, minced
- 1 onion, chopped

### Directions:

- Melt butter in a pan over medium heat.
- Add onion and garlic and sauté until onion is softened. Transfer to the soup maker.

- Add remaining ingredients except for milk to the soup maker and stir well.
- Seal soup maker with lid and cook on smooth mode for 10 minutes.
- Add milk and stir well.
- Serve and enjoy.

**Nutritional Value (Amount per Serving):**

- Calories 183
- Fat 7.2 g
- Carbohydrates 26.5 g
- Sugar 11.7 g
- Protein 7.5 g
- Cholesterol 20 mg

# 96-Tomato Eggplant Soup

**Time: 40 minutes**

**Serve: 4**

**Ingredients:**

- 1 medium eggplant, diced
- 1 tsp dried basil
- 1 tsp oregano
- 4 cup chicken stock
- 1 tbsp olive oil
- 5 garlic cloves, smashed
- 1 onion, chopped
- 4 large tomatoes, sliced
- Pepper
- Salt

**Directions:**

- Preheat the oven to 218 C/ 425 F.
- Place eggplant, garlic, onion, and tomatoes on a baking tray. Drizzle with oil and season with salt and pepper.

- Roast in preheated oven for 25 minutes.
- Transfer roasted eggplant, garlic, onion, and tomatoes to the soup maker.
- Add remaining ingredients to the soup maker and stir well.
- Seal soup maker with lid and cook on smooth mode for 10 minutes.
- Season soup with salt and pepper.
- Serve and enjoy.

**Nutritional Value (Amount per Serving):**

- Calories 119
- Fat 4.7 g
- Carbohydrates 18.6 g
- Sugar 10.2 g
- Protein 4 g
- Cholesterol 0 mg

# 97-Lebanese Eggplant Soup

**Time: 35 minutes**

**Serve: 4**

**Ingredients:**

- 1 medium eggplant; poke a few holes in the eggplant
- 3 cups chicken stock
- 1 tsp garlic, minced
- 1 onion, sliced
- 2 tbsp olive oil
- 1/4 tsp Italian seasoning
- Pepper
- Salt

**Directions:**

- Preheat the grill.
- Place eggplant on hot grill and grill for 10 minutes. Turn every 2-3 minutes.
- Remove eggplant from grill and set aside to cool.
- Once the eggplant is cook then peel and discard skin. Roughly chop the eggplant and set aside.

- Heat oil in a pan over medium heat.
- Add onion and sauté until onion is softened. Add garlic and sauté for 30 seconds.
- Add eggplant, sautéed onion and garlic to the soup maker.
- Add remaining ingredients to the soup maker and stir well.
- Seal soup maker with lid and cook on smooth mode for 15 minutes.
- Serve and enjoy.

**Nutritional Value (Amount per Serving):**

- Calories 109
- Fat 7.8 g
- Carbohydrates 10.1 g
- Sugar 5.2 g
- Protein 2 g
- Cholesterol 0 mg

# 98-Spicy Pumpkin Soup

**Time: 30 minutes**

**Serve: 4**

## Ingredients:

- 1 1/2 lb pumpkin, chopped
- 4 cups chicken stock
- 1 tsp chili powder
- 1/2 tsp cumin powder
- 1/2 tsp coriander powder
- 1/2 tsp garlic, crushed
- 1 onion, chopped
- 1 tbsp olive oil
- Pepper
- Salt

## Directions:

- Heat oil in a pan over medium heat.
- Add onion and sauté for 2-3 minutes. Add garlic and sauté for 30 seconds.

- Add sautéed onion and garlic to the soup maker.
- Add remaining ingredients to the soup maker and stir well.
- Seal soup maker with lid and cook on smooth mode for 21 minutes.
- Serve and enjoy.

**Nutritional Value (Amount per Serving):**

- Calories 112
- Fat 4.7 g
- Carbohydrates 17.7 g
- Sugar 7.6 g
- Protein 3 g
- Cholesterol 0 mg

# 99-Spicy Sweet Potato Soup

**Time: 30 minutes**

**Serve: 6**

**Ingredients:**

- 1 1/2 lbs sweet potato, peeled and chopped
- 4 cups vegetable stock
- 2 carrots, chopped
- 2 tsp chipotle chili paste
- 1/2 tsp garlic, crushed
- 1 onion, chopped
- 1 tbsp olive oil
- Pepper
- Salt

**Directions:**

- Heat oil in a pan over medium heat.
- Add onion and garlic and sauté for 2-3 minutes. Transfer to the soup maker.
- Add remaining ingredients to the soup maker and stir well.

- Seal soup maker with lid and cook on smooth mode for 21 minutes.
- Serve and enjoy.

**Nutritional Value (Amount per Serving):**

- Calories 143
- Fat 2.6 g
- Carbohydrates 27.9 g
- Sugar 9.6 g
- Protein 2.9 g
- Cholesterol 0 mg

# 100-Poblano Corn Soup

**Time: 30 minutes**

**Serve: 6**

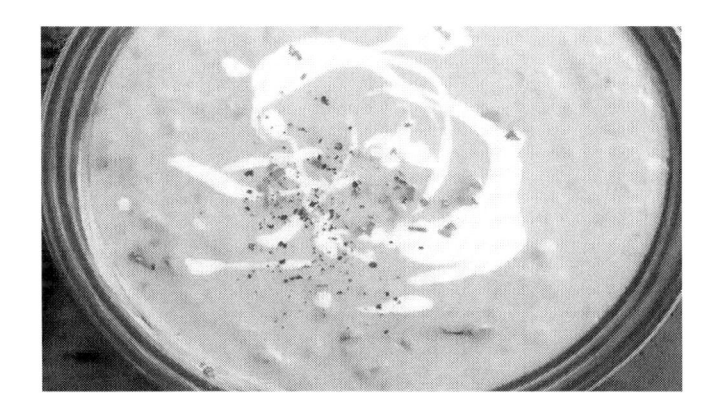

## Ingredients:

- 3 1/2 cups corn
- 1 cup milk
- 2 cups vegetable stock
- 1/2 tsp paprika
- 1 medium onion, chopped
- 1/2 tsp garlic, minced
- 1 tbsp olive oil
- 2 small poblano peppers, chopped
- 1 lime juice
- Pepper
- Salt

**Directions:**

- Heat oil in a pan over medium heat.
- Add onion and garlic and sauté until onion is softened. Transfer to the soup maker.
- Add remaining ingredients except milk and lime juice to the soup maker and stir well.
- Seal soup maker with lid and cook on smooth mode for 20 minutes.
- Add milk and lime juice and stir well.
- Season soup with salt and pepper.
- Serve and enjoy.

**Nutritional Value (Amount per Serving):**

- Calories 131
- Fat 4.3 g
- Carbohydrates 22.1 g
- Sugar 6.1 g
- Protein 4.7 g
- Cholesterol 3 mg

# 101-Spicy Cabbage Soup

**Time: 38 minutes**

**Serve: 6**

## Ingredients:

- 1 small cabbage head, chopped
- 2 tbsp tomato paste
- 1/2 tsp thyme
- 1 tsp fennel seeds
- 4 cups vegetable stock
- 14 oz can tomatoes, chopped
- 1 jalapeno pepper, chopped
- 1 onion, diced
- 1 celery stalk, diced
- 1 carrot, chopped

## Directions:

- Add all ingredients into the soup maker and stir well.
- Seal soup maker with lid and cook on chunky mode for 28 minutes.

- Serve and enjoy.

**Nutritional Value (Amount per Serving):**

- Calories 40
- Fat 0.2 g
- Carbohydrates 9 g
- Sugar 5.2 g
- Protein 1.7 g
- Cholesterol 0 mg

# 102-Nutmeg Pumpkin Soup

**Time: 26 minutes**

**Serve: 4**

### Ingredients:

- 2 cups pumpkin puree
- 1/4 tsp ground nutmeg
- 1 cup of coconut milk
- 4 cups of water

### Directions:

- Add all ingredients into the soup maker and stir well.
- Seal soup maker with lid and cook on smooth mode for 21 minutes.
- Serve and enjoy.

### Nutritional Value (Amount per Serving):

- Calories 180
- Fat 14 g
- Carbohydrates 13 g
- Sugar 6 g
- Protein 2 g
- Cholesterol 42 mg

# 103-Cauliflower Cheese Soup

**Time: 30 minutes**

**Serve: 6**

**Ingredients:**

- 3 cups cauliflower florets
- 3 cups vegetable stock
- 1/2 tbsp fresh thyme, chopped
- 1 tbsp garlic, minced
- 3.5 oz cream cheese
- 1/2 cup heavy cream
- 2 tbsp olive oil
- 2 tbsp butter
- Pepper
- Salt

## Directions:

- Preheat the oven to 425 F/ 218 C.
- Spread cauliflower florets onto the baking tray and drizzle with oil. Season with salt and pepper.
- Roast in preheated oven for 10 minutes.
- Add roasted cauliflower, stock, thyme, garlic, and butter to the soup maker.
- Seal soup maker with lid and cook on smooth mode for 15 minutes.
- Add heavy cream and cream cheese and stir well.
- Season soup with salt and pepper.
- Serve and enjoy.

## Nutritional Value (Amount per Serving):

- Calories 185
- Fat 19 g
- Carbohydrates 5 g
- Sugar 2 g
- Protein 2 g
- Cholesterol 42 mg

# 104-Cauliflower Chicken Soup

**Time: 30 minutes**

**Serve: 4**

**Ingredients:**

- 2 cups chicken, cooked and shredded
- 1 1/2 cup cauliflower rice, cooked
- 1/2 tsp onion powder
- 1/4 cup heavy cream
- 14 oz chicken stock
- 4 oz cream cheese, cubed
- 1 tbsp garlic, minced
- 2 tbsp butter
- Salt

**Directions:**

- Add all ingredients into the soup maker and stir well.
- Seal soup maker with lid and cook on chunky mode for 25 minutes.
- Serve and enjoy.

**Nutritional Value (Amount per Serving):**

- Calories 300
- Fat 21 g
- Carbohydrates 4 g
- Sugar 1 g
- Protein 23 g
- Cholesterol 110 mg

# 105-Curried Cauliflower Soup

**Time:** 15 minutes

**Serve:** 2

## Ingredients:

- 1/2 lb cauliflower florets
- 1 1/2 tsp curry powder
- 1/2 tsp garlic clove, minced
- 1/2 onion, minced
- 1 1/4 cup water
- Pepper
- Salt

## Directions:

- Add all ingredients into the soup maker and stir well.
- Seal soup maker with lid and cook on smooth mode for 15 minutes.
- Season soup with salt and pepper.
- Serve and enjoy.

## Nutritional Value (Amount per Serving):

- Calories 45
- Fat 0.5 g
- Carbohydrates 10 g
- Sugar 3 g
- Protein 2 g
- Cholesterol 0 mg

# 106-Cheesy Cauliflower Soup

**Time: 26 minutes**

**Serve: 6**

## Ingredients:

- 12 oz cauliflower, cut into florets
- 4 oz cream cheese, cut into cubes
- 5 cups chicken broth
- 1 cup heavy cream
- 1 cup cheddar cheese, grated
- Pepper
- Salt

## Directions:

- Add cauliflower, chicken broth, onion, pepper, and salt to the soup maker and stir well.
- Seal soup maker with lid and cook on smooth mode for 21 minutes.
- Stir in cream, cheddar cheese, and cream cheese.
- Stir well and serve.

## Nutritional Value (Amount per Serving):

- Calories 140
- Fat 10 g
- Carbohydrates 15 g
- Sugar 8 g
- Protein 1 g
- Cholesterol 0 mg

# 107-Herb Asparagus Soup

**Time: 50 minutes**

**Serve: 6**

### Ingredients:

- 2 lbs fresh asparagus, cut off the woody stems
- 1 tsp dried thyme
- 1/2 tsp oregano
- 1/2 tsp sage
- 1 1/2 cups water
- 1 cauliflower head, cut into florets
- 1/4 tsp lime zest
- 2 tbsp lime juice
- 14 oz coconut milk
- 1 tbsp garlic, minced
- 1 leek, sliced
- 3 tbsp olive oil
- Salt

## Directions:

- Preheat the oven to 400 F/ 200 C.
- Arrange asparagus on a baking tray. Drizzle with 2 tablespoons of oil and sprinkle with salt, thyme, oregano, and sage.
- Roast in preheated oven for 20 minutes.
- Heat remaining oil to the pan over medium heat.
- Add garlic and leek and sauté for 2-3 minutes. Transfer to the soup maker.
- Add asparagus to the soup maker.
- Add remaining ingredients to the soup maker and stir well.
- Seal soup maker with lid and cook on smooth mode for 21 minutes.
- Serve and enjoy.

## Nutritional Value (Amount per Serving):

- Calories 266
- Fat 23 g
- Carbohydrates 15 g
- Sugar 6 g
- Protein 6.1 g
- Cholesterol 0 mg

# 108-Nutritious White Bean Soup

**Time: 38 minutes**

**Serve: 6**

## Ingredients:

- 2 cups white beans, rinsed
- 3 cups almond milk
- 3 garlic cloves, minced
- 2 celery stalks, diced
- 1 onion, chopped
- 1/4 tsp cayenne pepper
- 1 tsp dried oregano
- 1/2 tsp fresh rosemary, chopped
- 3 cups of water
- 1 tbsp olive oil
- 1/2 tsp sea salt

## Directions:

- Heat oil in a pan over medium heat.
- Add carrots, celery, and onion sauté until softened, about 5 minutes.
- Add garlic and sauté for a minute. Transfer to the soup maker.
- Add remaining ingredients to the soup maker and stir well.
- Seal soup maker with lid and cook on chunky mode for 28 minutes.
- Serve and enjoy.

**Nutritional Value (Amount per Serving):**

- Calories 275
- Fat 5 g
- Carbohydrates 44 g
- Sugar 2 g
- Protein 16 g
- Cholesterol 0 mg

# 109-Spinach Green Lentil Soup

**Time: 38 minutes**

**Serve: 4**

### Ingredients:

- 1 1/2 cups green lentils, rinsed and soaked for 1 hour
- 14 oz tomatoes, diced
- 3 garlic cloves, minced
- 2 celery stalks, chopped
- 4 cups baby spinach
- 4 cups of water
- 1 tsp Italian seasoning
- 2 tsp fresh thyme
- 1 carrot, chopped
- 1 onion, chopped
- Pepper
- Salt

## Directions:

- Add all ingredients into the soup maker and stir everything well.
- Seal soup maker with lid and cook on chunky mode for 28 minutes.
- Season soup with salt and pepper.
- Serve and enjoy.

## Nutritional Value (Amount per Serving):

- Calories 306
- Fat 1.5 g
- Carbohydrates 53.7 g
- Sugar 6.4 g
- Protein 21 g
- Cholesterol 1 mg

# 110-Spicy Carrot Soup

**Time: 30 minutes**

**Serve: 6**

**Ingredients:**

- 8 large carrots, peeled and chopped
- 1/2 garlic, crushed
- 1 tbsp red curry paste
- 1/4 cup olive oil
- 1 1/2 cups water
- 14 oz coconut milk
- 1 onion, chopped
- Pepper
- Salt

**Directions:**

- Heat oil in a pan over medium heat.
- Add onion and garlic and sauté until onion is softened. Transfer to the soup maker.

- Add remaining ingredients to the soup maker and stir well.
- Seal soup maker with lid and cook on smooth mode for 21 minutes.
- Season soup with salt and pepper.
- Serve and enjoy.

**Nutritional Value (Amount per Serving):**

- Calories 265
- Fat 22 g
- Carbohydrates 13 g
- Protein 5 g
- Sugar 4 g
- Cholesterol 20 mg

# 111- Curried Zucchini Soup

**Time: 26 minutes**

**Serve: 5**

### Ingredients:

- 5 cups zucchini, chopped
- 16 oz water
- 14 oz coconut milk
- 1 tbsp Thai curry paste

### Directions:

- Add all ingredients into the soup maker and stir well.
- Seal soup maker with lid and cook on smooth mode for 21 minutes.
- Serve and enjoy.

### Nutritional Value (Amount per Serving):

- Calories 122
- Fat 9 g
- Carbohydrates 6 g
- Protein 4 g
- Sugar 3 g
- Cholesterol 0 mg

# 112-Creamy Cauliflower Soup

**Time: 30 minutes**

**Serve: 6**

## Ingredients:

- 1 lb cauliflower florets
- 3 garlic cloves, minced
- 1 onion, sliced
- 3 cups of water
- 1 cup of coconut milk
- 1 medium fennel bulbs, chopped
- 1 tbsp olive oil
- 2 tsp sea salt

## Directions:

- Heat oil in a pan over medium heat.
- Add onion and garlic and sauté until onion is softened. Transfer to the soup maker.
- Add remaining ingredients to the soup maker and stir well.

- Seal soup maker with lid and cook on smooth mode for 21 minutes.
- Serve and enjoy.

**Nutritional Value (Amount per Serving):**

- Calories 170
- Fat 12 g
- Carbohydrates 11 g
- Protein 5 g
- Sugar 4 g
- Cholesterol 0 mg

# 113-Cheesy Broccoli Soup

**Time: 38 minutes**

**Serve: 4**

## Ingredients:

- 4 1/2 cups broccoli florets
- 1/4 cup cream cheese
- 1/4 cup butter
- 1/2 cup heavy cream
- 2 cups chicken stock
- 1 1/2 cups cheddar cheese
- 1/2 cup mozzarella cheese
- Pepper
- Salt

## Directions:

- Add all ingredients except cheddar cheese and mozzarella cheese into the soup maker and stir well.
- Seal soup maker with lid and cook on chunky mode for 28 minutes.

- Add cheddar cheese and mozzarella cheese and stir well.
- Season soup with salt and pepper.
- Serve and enjoy.

**Nutritional Value (Amount per Serving):**

- Calories 426
- Fat 36 g
- Carbohydrates 7 g
- Sugar 2 g
- Protein 15 g
- Cholesterol 112 mg

# 114-Coconut Garlic Mushroom Soup

**Time: 30 minutes**

**Serve: 5**

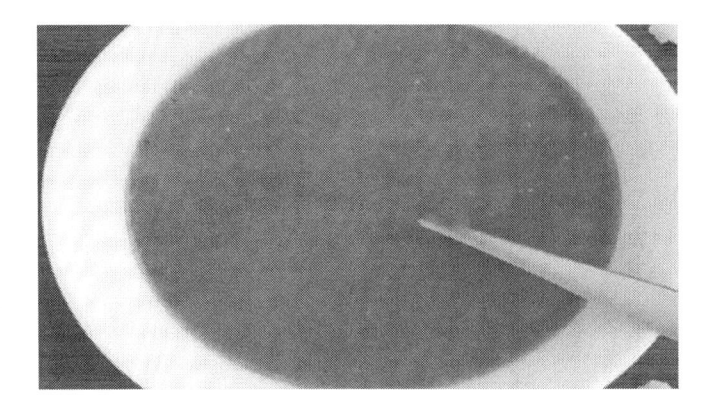

**Ingredients:**

- 20 oz mushrooms, sliced
- 1 cup of coconut milk
- 1 cup heavy cream
- 1 tbsp olive oil
- 2 cups vegetable broth
- 5 garlic cloves, minced
- 1/2 onion, diced
- Pepper
- Salt

**Directions:**

- Heat oil in a pan over medium heat.
- Add mushrooms and onions and sauté for 5 minutes.
- Add garlic and sauté for a minute. Transfer to the soup maker.

- Add remaining ingredients to the soup maker and stir well.
- Seal soup maker with lid and cook on smooth mode for 21 minutes.
- Serve and enjoy.

**Nutritional Value (Amount per Serving):**

- Calories 251
- Fat 23 g
- Carbohydrates 9 g
- Sugar 4 g
- Protein 5 g
- Cholesterol 32 mg

# 115-Cabbage Coconut Soup

**Time: 30 minutes**

**Serve: 4**

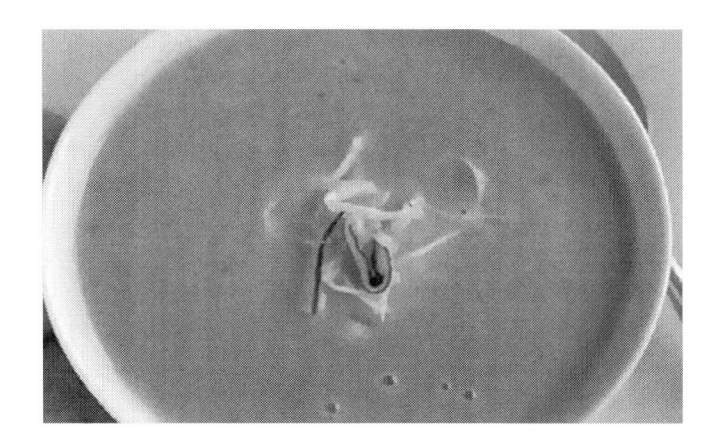

**Ingredients:**

- 1 small cabbage head
- 2 tbsp coconut oil
- 1 tsp cumin powder
- 2 tsp turmeric powder
- 2 garlic cloves, chopped
- 3 cups vegetable stock
- 1/4 cup coconut milk
- 1/2 tsp pepper
- 1/2 tsp salt

**Directions:**

- Heat oil in a pan over medium heat.
- Add cabbage and garlic and sauté for 5 minutes. Transfer to the soup maker.

- Add remaining ingredients to the soup maker and stir well.
- Seal soup maker with lid and cook on smooth mode for 21 minutes.
- Serve and enjoy.

**Nutritional Value (Amount per Serving):**

- Calories 150
- Fat 11 g
- Carbohydrates 13 g
- Sugar 6 g
- Protein 3 g
- Cholesterol 0 mg

## 116-Avocado Soup

**Time: 20 minutes**

**Serve: 4**

### Ingredients:

- 2 avocados, pitted
- 1/2 lime juice
- 1 tsp garlic powder
- 1/3 cup fresh cilantro, chopped
- 4 cups chicken stock
- 1/2 lb bacon, cooked and chopped
- Pepper
- Salt

### Directions:

- Add all ingredients except lime juice and bacon to the soup maker and stir well.
- Seal soup maker with lid and cook on smooth mode for 15 minutes.
- Add bacon and lime juice and stir well.

- Season with salt and pepper.
- Serve and enjoy.

**Nutritional Value (Amount per Serving):**

- Calories 350
- Fat 25 g
- Carbohydrates 4.1 g
- Sugar 1 g
- Protein 22 g
- Cholesterol 0 mg

# 117-Broccoli Avocado Soup

**Time: 20 minutes**

**Serve: 3**

## Ingredients:

- 4 cup broccoli florets
- 2 cups vegetable broth
- 1 small avocado, peeled and sliced
- 1/2 tsp nutmeg

## Directions:

- Add all ingredients to the soup maker and stir well.
- Seal soup maker with lid and cook on smooth mode for 15 minutes.
- Serve and enjoy.

## Nutritional Value (Amount per Serving):

- Calories 90
- Fat 3 g
- Carbohydrates 10 g
- Sugar 2.6 g
- Protein 7 g
- Cholesterol 0 mg

# 118-Chicken Taco Soup

**Time: 33 minutes**

**Serve: 4**

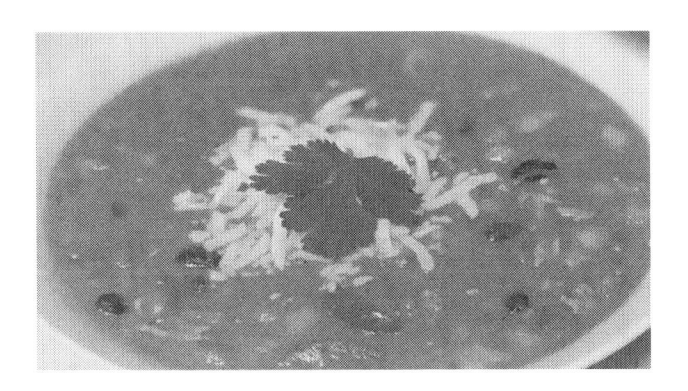

**Ingredients:**

- 2 cups chicken breasts, cooked and shredded
- 1/2 cup heavy cream
- 8 oz cream cheese
- 1/2 tbsp taco seasoning
- 10 oz can tomatoes
- 1 tbsp olive oil
- 3 cups chicken stock
- Salt

**Directions:**

- Add all ingredients except heavy cream and cream cheese into the soup maker and stir well.
- Seal soup maker with lid and cook on chunky mode for 28 minutes.
- Add heavy cream and cream cheese and stir well.
- Serve and enjoy.

**Nutritional Value (Amount per Serving):**

- Calories 440
- Fat 32 g
- Carbohydrates 7.6 g
- Sugar 3 g
- Protein 30 g
- Cholesterol 155 mg

# 119-Almond Broccoli Cheese Soup

**Time: 26 minutes**

**Serve: 6**

### Ingredients:

- 8 oz broccoli florets
- 1/2 cup heavy cream
- 3 cups chicken stock
- 3 tbsp almonds, chopped
- 10 oz goat cheese, crumbled
- 1 tsp salt

### Directions:

- Add broccoli, stock, and salt to the soup maker and stir well.
- Seal soup maker with lid and cook on smooth mode for 21 minutes.
- Add heavy cream and cheese and stir well.
- Garnish with almonds and serve.

**Nutritional Value (Amount per Serving):**

- Calories 284
- Fat 22 g
- Carbohydrates 4 g
- Sugar 2.2 g
- Protein 15 g
- Cholesterol 63 mg

# 120-Healthy Chickpea Lentil Soup

**Time: 38 minutes**

**Serve: 6**

**Ingredients:**

- 1 cup dry red lentils, rinsed and soaked for 2 hours
- 1/4 tsp cayenne powder
- 1/4 tsp coriander powder
- 1/2 tsp chili powder
- 1/4 tsp cinnamon
- 1/4 tsp paprika
- 1/4 tsp turmeric
- 2 tbsp olive oil
- 1 tsp fresh ginger, minced
- 3 garlic cloves, minced
- 14 oz can chickpeas
- 1 tbsp fresh lemon juice
- 2 cups of water
- 4 cups vegetable stock
- 14 oz can tomatoes, diced

- 1 cup carrot, diced
- 1 cup onion, diced
- 1 1/2 tsp sea salt

**Directions:**

- Heat oil in a pan over medium heat.
- Add carrots, onion, ginger, and garlic and sauté until onion is softened. Transfer to the soup maker.
- Add remaining ingredients to the soup maker and stir well.
- Seal soup maker with lid and cook on chunky mode for 28 minutes.
- Serve and enjoy.

**Nutritional Value (Amount per Serving):**

- Calories 275
- Fat 6 g
- Carbohydrates 43 g
- Sugar 5 g
- Protein 13 g
- Cholesterol 0 mg

# 121-Roasted Pepper Soup

**Time: 30 minutes**

**Serve: 8**

## Ingredients:

- 24 oz roasted red bell peppers
- 4 cups vegetable stock
- 1 onion, chopped
- 2 garlic cloves, chopped
- 1 cauliflower head, chopped
- 2 tbsp olive oil
- 8 oz feta cheese, crumbled
- 1 tsp parsley
- 6 oz can tomato paste
- Pepper
- Salt

## Directions:

- Heat oil in a pan over medium heat.
- Add onion, garlic, and cauliflower and sauté until onion is softened. Transfer to the soup maker.
- Add remaining ingredients except cheese to the soup maker and stir well.
- Seal soup maker with lid and cook on smooth mode for 21 minutes.
- Add cheese and stir well.
- Serve and enjoy.

## Nutritional Value (Amount per Serving):

- Calories 170
- Fat 10 g
- Carbohydrates 14 g
- Sugar 9 g
- Protein 5 g
- Cholesterol 25 mg

# 122-Chickpea Chicken Soup

**Time: 38 minutes**

**Serve: 4**

**Ingredients:**

- 2 chicken breasts, boneless, cooked and shredded
- 14 oz can chickpeas, drained and rinsed
- 2 celery stalks, diced
- 5 cups spinach
- 5 cups chicken stock
- 1/4 cup fresh lemon juice
- 1 tsp garlic powder
- 1/4 tsp cinnamon
- 1 onion, diced
- 2 carrots, diced
- Pepper
- Salt

## Directions:

- Add all ingredients to the soup maker and stir well.
- Seal soup maker with lid and cook on chunky mode for 28 minutes.
- Season soup with salt and pepper
- Serve and enjoy.

## Nutritional Value (Amount per Serving):

- Calories 330
- Fat 8.2 g
- Carbohydrates 35 g
- Sugar 5 g
- Protein 31 g
- Cholesterol 65 mg

# 123-Cheesy Asparagus Soup

**Time: 30 minutes**

**Serve: 6**

**Ingredients:**

- 2 lbs asparagus, cut the ends and chop into ½-inch pieces
- 2 oz parmesan cheese, grated
- 1/2 cup heavy cream
- 1/4 cup onion, chopped
- 4 cups vegetable stock
- 2 tbsp olive oil
- 3 garlic cloves, minced
- Pepper
- Salt

**Directions:**

- Heat oil in a pan over medium heat.
- Add onion and garlic and sauté until onion is softened. Transfer to the soup maker.
- Add remaining ingredients except cheese to the soup maker and stir well.
- Seal soup maker with lid and cook on smooth mode for 21 minutes.
- Add cheese and stir well.
- Serve and enjoy.

**Nutritional Value (Amount per Serving):**

- Calories 145
- Fat 12 g
- Carbohydrates 8.8 g
- Sugar 4 g
- Protein 6 g
- Cholesterol 20 mg

# 124-Basil Celery Soup

**Time: 30 minutes**

**Serve: 4**

**Ingredients:**

- 3 cups celery, chopped
- 1/4 cup onion, chopped
- 1 tbsp garlic, chopped
- 1 tbsp olive oil
- 1 cup vegetable broth
- 5 oz cream cheese
- 1 1/2 tbsp fresh basil, chopped
- Pepper
- Salt

**Directions:**

- Heat oil in a pan over medium heat.
- Add onion, garlic, and celery and sauté for 4-5 minutes. Transfer to the soup maker.

- Add remaining ingredients except cream cheese and basil to the soup maker. Stir well.
- Seal soup maker with lid and cook on smooth mode for 21 minutes.
- Season soup with salt and pepper.
- Serve and enjoy.

**Nutritional Value (Amount per Serving):**

- Calories 182
- Fat 16 g
- Carbohydrates 5 g
- Sugar 1 g
- Protein 4.7 g
- Cholesterol 39 mg

# 125-Vegan Mushroom Soup

**Time: 30 minutes**

**Serves: 4**

**Ingredients:**

- 8 oz shiitake mushrooms, sliced
- 8 oz crimini mushrooms, sliced
- 1 carrot, peeled and chopped
- 1 large celery stalk, chopped
- 1 onion, chopped
- 2 tsp olive oil
- 2/3 cup coconut milk
- 3 cups vegetable broth
- 1 tsp dried thyme
- 3 garlic cloves, minced
- Pepper
- Salt

## Directions:

- Heat oil in a pan over medium heat.
- Add carrots, celery, and onion and sauté for 3-4 minutes. Transfer to the soup maker.
- Add remaining ingredients except for coconut milk to the soup maker and stir well.
- Seal soup maker with lid and cook on smooth mode for 21 minutes.
- Add coconut milk and stir well. Season soup with salt and pepper.
- Serve and enjoy.

## Nutritional Value (Amount per Serving):

- Calories 211
- Fat 13 g
- Carbohydrates 18 g
- Sugar 7 g
- Protein 7 g
- Cholesterol 40 mg

# 126-Coconut Celery Soup

**Time: 26 minutes**

**Serve: 4**

**Ingredients:**

- 6 cups celery stalk, chopped
- 1/2 tsp dill
- 1 cup of coconut milk
- 2 cups vegetable stock
- 1 onion, chopped
- 1/4 tsp salt

**Directions:**

- Add all ingredients into the soup maker and stir well.
- Seal soup maker with lid and cook on smooth mode for 21 minutes.
- Serve and enjoy.

**Nutritional Value (Amount per Serving):**

- Calories 179
- Fat 15 g
- Carbohydrates 11 g
- Sugar 6 g
- Protein 2 g
- Cholesterol 13 mg

# 127-Celery Broccoli Soup

**Time: 38 minutes**

**Serves: 4**

## Ingredients:

- 2 cups broccoli florets, chopped
- 1 onion, diced
- 1 cup coconut cream
- 32 oz vegetable broth
- 2 tbsp olive oil
- 2 small carrots, diced
- 2 celery stalk, sliced
- 1/2 tsp pepper
- 1/2 tsp salt

## Directions:

- Heat oil in a pan over medium heat.
- Add onion, carrots, and celery and sauté until onion is softened. Transfer to the soup maker.

- Add remaining ingredients except for coconut cream to the soup maker and stir well.
- Seal soup maker with lid and cook on chunky mode for 28 minutes.
- Add coconut cream and stir well.
- Serve and enjoy.

**Nutritional Value (Amount per Serving):**

- Calories 273
- Fat 22.8 g
- Carbohydrates 12 g
- Sugar 5 g
- Protein 7 g
- Cholesterol 16 mg

# 128-Pepper Zucchini Soup

**Time: 30 minutes**

**Serve: 4**

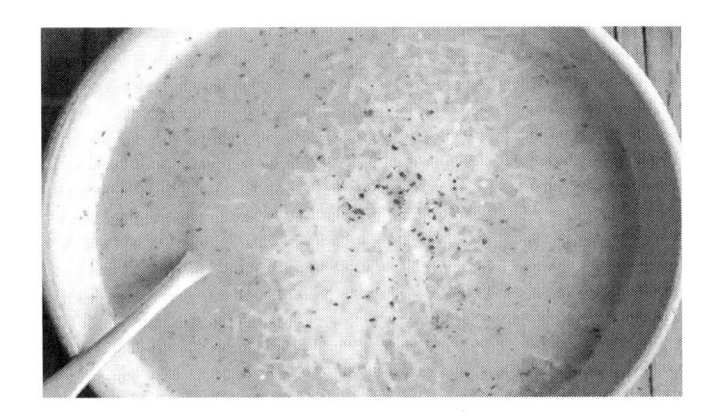

**Ingredients:**

- 1 zucchini, chopped
- 1 cup of coconut milk
- 1 cup of water
- 1 tbsp olive oil
- 1 bell pepper, chopped
- 2 carrots, chopped
- Salt

**Directions:**

- Heat oil in a pan over medium heat.
- Add vegetables and cook for 5 minutes. Transfer to the soup maker.
- Add remaining ingredients to the soup maker and stir well.

- Seal soup maker with lid and cook on smooth mode for 21 minutes.
- Season soup with salt and pepper.
- Serve and enjoy.

**Nutritional Value (Amount per Serving):**

- Calories 202
- Fat 18 g
- Carbohydrates 10 g
- Sugar 5 g
- Protein 2 g
- Cholesterol 18 mg

# 129-Tomato Carrot Soup

**Time: 26 minutes**

**Serve: 4**

**Ingredients:**

- 4 medium carrots, peeled and chopped
- 1 tbsp turmeric
- 1 cup of coconut milk
- 14.5 oz can tomatoes, diced
- 1 tsp ground cumin
- 1 tsp ground coriander

**Directions:**

- Add all ingredients into the soup maker and stir well.
- Seal soup maker with lid and cook on smooth mode for 21 minutes.
- Serve and enjoy.

**Nutritional Value (Amount per Serving):**

- Calories 193
- Fat 14 g
- Carbohydrates 15 g
- Sugar 8 g
- Protein 3 g
- Cholesterol 14 mg

# 130-Healthy Veggie Soup

**Time: 38 minutes**

**Serves: 4**

## Ingredients:

- 4.5 oz fresh spinach, chopped
- 2 yellow peppers, chopped
- 2 carrots, sliced
- 1 tbsp olive oil
- 1 tsp dried mixed herbs
- 3 cups vegetable stock
- 14 oz tomatoes, chopped
- Pepper
- Salt

## Directions:

- Heat oil in a pan over medium heat.
- Add carrots and peppers and cook until softened. Transfer to the soup maker.

- Add remaining ingredients to the soup maker and stir well.
- Seal soup maker with lid and cook on chunky mode for 28 minutes.
- Season soup with salt and pepper.
- Serve and enjoy.

**Nutritional Value (Amount per Serving):**

- Calories 102
- Fat 5 g
- Carbohydrates 15 g
- Sugar 5 g
- Protein 3 g
- Cholesterol 32 mg

## 131-Chicken Enchilada Soup

**Time: 38 minutes**

**Serve: 2**

### Ingredients:

- 1 chicken breast, boneless, cooked, and shredded
- 1 garlic clove, chopped
- 1/2 onion, chopped
- 1 potato, peeled and diced
- 2 cups chicken broth
- 4 cups butternut squash, peeled and diced
- 1.5 oz can green chilies
- 4 oz tomato sauce
- 14 oz cannellini beans, drained
- 1 tsp cumin
- 1 tbsp taco seasoning
- 1/4 cup cheddar cheese, grated
- 1/2 bell pepper, chopped
- Pepper
- Salt

## Directions:

- Add all ingredients into the soup maker and stir well.
- Seal soup maker with lid and cook on chunky mode for 28 minutes.
- Season soup with salt and pepper.
- Serve and enjoy.

## Nutritional Value (Amount per Serving):

- Calories 685
- Fat 12 g
- Carbohydrates 93 g
- Sugar 13 g
- Protein 50 g
- Cholesterol 30 mg

## 132-Sweet Potato Soup

**Time: 26 minutes**

**Serve: 6**

### Ingredients:

- 28 oz can tomatoes, crushed
- 2/3 cup almond butter
- 2 large sweet potatoes, peeled and diced
- 5 cups of water
- 1/4 tsp cayenne pepper
- 1 tbsp curry powder
- 1/4 cup almonds, toasted and chopped
- Salt

### Directions:

- Add all ingredients except almonds to the soup maker and stir well.
- Seal soup maker with lid and cook on smooth mode for 21 minutes.

- Garnish with chopped almonds and serve.

**Nutritional Value (Amount per Serving):**

- Calories 131
- Fat 5 g
- Carbohydrates 19 g
- Sugar 7 g
- Protein 3 g
- Cholesterol 26 mg

## 133-Asian Pepper Soup

**Time: 15 minutes**

**Serves: 2**

### Ingredients:

- 4 red bell pepper, diced
- 2 tsp turmeric
- 1 cup unsweetened coconut milk
- 1 tbsp ginger, grated
- 1 red chili pepper
- 1 leek, green part only
- 2 oz chia seeds
- 1/4 tsp pepper
- 1/4 tsp salt

### Directions:

- Add all ingredients except chia seeds into the soup maker.
- Seal soup maker with lid and cook on smooth mode for 10 minutes.

- Add chia seeds and stir well.
- Serve and enjoy.

**Nutritional Value (Amount per Serving):**

- Calories 275
- Fat 11 g
- Carbohydrates 34 g
- Sugar 14 g
- Protein 9 g
- Cholesterol 12 mg

# 134-Pesto Zucchini Soup

**Time: 26 minutes**

**Serves: 8**

**Ingredients:**

- 2 large zucchini, chopped
- 2 cups potatoes, peeled and diced
- 2 medium tomatoes, chopped
- 1 bell pepper, chopped
- 2 tbsp basil pesto
- 6 cups of water
- Pepper
- Salt

**Directions:**

- Add all ingredients except basil pesto into the soup maker and stir well.
- Seal soup maker with lid and cook on smooth mode for 21 minutes.
- Add basil pesto and stir well.

- Season soup with salt and pepper.
- Serve and enjoy.

**Nutritional Value (Amount per Serving):**

- Calories 49
- Fat 0.3 g
- Carbohydrates 11 g
- Sugar 3.4 g
- Protein 2.1 g
- Cholesterol 10 mg

# 135-Yummy Chicken Tomato Soup

**Time: 38 minutes**

**Serve: 6**

## Ingredients:

- 30 oz can roasted tomatoes
- 14 oz coconut milk
- 1 1/2 lbs chicken thighs, boneless, cooked and shredded
- 1/3 cup fresh basil
- 1 cup of water
- 1/4 tsp pepper
- 1 tsp salt

## Directions:

- Add all ingredients into the soup maker and stir well.
- Seal soup maker with lid and cook on chunky mode for 28 minutes.
- Serve and enjoy.

## Nutritional Value (Amount per Serving):

- Calories 515
- Fat 31 g
- Carbohydrates 10 g
- Sugar 5 g
- Protein 46 g
- Cholesterol 10 mg

# 136-Chili Chicken Soup

**Time: 38 minutes**

**Serve: 6**

**Ingredients:**

- 2 lbs chicken breast, boneless, cooked, and shredded
- 1 tbsp paprika
- 2 tsp cumin
- 24 oz can tomatoes, diced
- 1 tbsp oregano
- 1/4 cup green onion, chopped
- 4 oz can green chilies, chopped
- 1 cup of water

**Directions:**

- Add all ingredients into the soup maker and stir well.
- Seal soup maker with lid and cook on chunky mode for 28 minutes.
- Serve and enjoy.

**Nutritional Value (Amount per Serving):**

- Calories 251
- Fat 8 g
- Carbohydrates 8 g
- Sugar 4 g
- Protein 33 g
- Cholesterol 34 mg

# 137-Vegan Bean Soup

**Time: 33 minutes**

**Serve: 4**

## Ingredients:

- 2 cups frozen corn
- 16 oz salsa
- 4 cups can black beans
- 1 tsp chili powder
- 1 tsp cumin
- 4 cups chicken stock
- 1 tsp salt

## Directions:

- Add all ingredients into the soup maker and stir well.
- Seal soup maker with lid and cook on chunky mode for 28 minutes.
- Serve and enjoy.

**Nutritional Value (Amount per Serving):**

- Calories 350
- Fat 2.9 g
- Carbohydrates 68.9 g
- Sugar 8.7 g
- Protein 19.1 g
- Cholesterol 0 mg

## 138-Cannellini Bean Soup

**Time: 33 minutes**

**Serves: 4**

**Ingredients:**

- 14 oz can cannellini beans, rinsed and drained
- 2 celery stalks, diced
- 3 cups vegetable stock
- 1 garlic cloves, minced
- 2 tbsp olive oil
- 14 oz can tomatoes crushed, drained
- 1 onion, diced
- 1 carrot, diced
- Pepper
- Salt

**Directions:**

- Add all ingredients into the soup maker and stir well.
- Seal soup maker with lid and cook on chunky mode for 28 minutes.

- Serve and enjoy.

**Nutritional Value (Amount per Serving):**

- Calories 285
- Fat 8 g
- Carbohydrates 45 g
- Sugar 2 g
- Protein 13.2 g
- Cholesterol 0 mg

# 139-Tasty Carrot Peanut Butter Soup

**Time: 26 minutes**

**Serve: 4**

## Ingredients:

- 8 carrots, peeled and chopped
- 14 oz coconut milk
- 1 1/2 cup chicken stock
- 1/4 cup peanut butter
- 1 tbsp curry paste
- 1 onion, chopped
- 3 garlic cloves, peeled
- Pepper
- Salt

## Directions:

- Add all ingredients into the soup maker and stir well.
- Seal soup maker with lid and cook on smooth mode for 21 minutes.
- Season soup with salt and pepper.

- Serve and enjoy.

**Nutritional Value (Amount per Serving):**

- Calories 416
- Fat 34 g
- Carbohydrates 25 g
- Sugar 12.3 g
- Protein 8.2 g
- Cholesterol 31 mg

# 140-Veggie Chicken Soup

**Time: 38 minutes**

**Serve: 6**

**Ingredients:**

- 2 chicken breasts, boneless, cooked and shredded
- 1/4 cup cabbage, shredded
- 1 cup of frozen green beans
- 1/4 cup frozen peas
- 1/2 cup frozen corn
- 2 celery stalk, chopped
- 1 carrot, peeled and cubed
- 1/2 tsp red pepper flakes
- 1/4 cup fresh parsley, chopped
- 1 tsp garlic powder
- 3 cups chicken broth
- 14 oz can tomatoes, diced
- 1/2 sweet potato, peeled and cubed
- 3 garlic cloves, minced
- 1/2 onion, chopped

- 1/2 tsp pepper
- 1 tsp salt

**Directions:**

- Add all ingredients into the soup maker and stir well.
- Seal soup maker with lid and cook on chunky mode for 28 minutes.
- Serve and enjoy.

**Nutritional Value (Amount per Serving):**

- Calories 171
- Fat 4.6 g
- Carbohydrates 13.9 g
- Sugar 5.4 g
- Protein 18.9 g
- Cholesterol 32 mg

# 141-Chicken Rice Noodle Soup

**Time: 20 minutes**

**Serve: 6**

**Ingredients:**

- 6 cups chicken, cooked and shredded
- 3 garlic cloves, minced
- 8 oz rice noodles
- 1 bell pepper, chopped
- 1 large carrot, peeled and sliced
- 6 cups chicken stock
- 2 celery stalks, sliced
- 3 tbsp rice vinegar
- 2 1/2 cups cabbage, shredded
- 2 tbsp fresh ginger, grated
- 2 tbsp soy sauce
- 1 onion, chopped
- 1/2 tsp pepper

**Directions:**

- Add all ingredients into the soup maker and stir well.
- Seal soup maker with lid and cook on chunky mode for 15 minutes.
- Serve and enjoy.

**Nutritional Value (Amount per Serving):**

- Calories 306
- Fat 5.1 g
- Carbohydrates 18.7 g
- Sugar 4.3 g
- Protein 43 g
- Cholesterol 12 mg

# 142-Pumpkin Spice Cauliflower Soup

**Time: 30 minutes**

**Serve: 4**

### Ingredients:

- 2 cups cauliflower florets
- 1 tsp pumpkin pie spice
- 5 cups chicken broth
- 3 tbsp olive oil
- 1 onion, chopped
- 1/4 tsp salt

### Directions:

- Heat oil in a pan over medium heat.
- Add onion and sauté until softened. Transfer to the soup maker.
- Add remaining ingredients to the soup maker and stir well.

- Seal soup maker with lid and cook on smooth mode for 21 minutes.
- Serve and enjoy.

**Nutritional Value (Amount per Serving):**

- Calories 163
- Fat 12.3 g
- Carbohydrates 6.7 g
- Sugar 3.3 g
- Protein 7.4 g
- Cholesterol 10 mg

# 143-Chicken Kale Soup

**Time: 33 minutes**

**Serve: 4**

## Ingredients:

- 2 cups chicken breast, cooked and chopped
- 4 cups vegetable broth
- 1 onion, diced
- 12 oz kale
- 2 tsp garlic, minced
- 1/2 tsp cinnamon
- 1 tsp salt

## Directions:

- Add all ingredients into the soup maker and stir well.
- Seal soup maker with lid and cook on chunky mode for 28 minutes.
- Serve and enjoy.

**Nutritional Value (Amount per Serving):**

- Calories 158
- Fat 2.8 g
- Carbohydrates 13 g
- Sugar 1.9 g
- Protein 19 g
- Cholesterol 6 mg

# 144-Mexican Chicken Soup

**Time: 38 minutes**

**Serve: 4**

**Ingredients:**

- 1 lb chicken breast, boneless, cooked and shredded
- 1 tsp coriander powder
- 2 cups bell pepper, chopped
- 1 tbsp garlic, minced
- 1 jalapeno pepper, diced
- 1 cup onion, diced
- 1 tbsp olive oil
- 1 tsp ground cumin
- 1 scallion, chopped
- 1 tbsp fresh lemon juice
- 2 cups chicken stock
- 14 oz can tomatoes, diced
- 1/4 tsp red pepper flakes
- 1 tsp salt

**Directions:**

- Heat oil in a pan over medium heat.
- Add garlic, onion, bell pepper, and jalapeno and sauté for 2 minutes. Transfer to the soup maker.
- Add remaining ingredients except lemon juice to the soup maker and stir well.
- Seal soup maker with lid and cook on chunky mode for 28 minutes.
- Add lemon juice and stir well.
- Serve and enjoy.

**Nutritional Value (Amount per Serving):**

- Calories 225
- Fat 7 g
- Carbohydrates 14 g
- Sugar 8 g
- Protein 25 g
- Cholesterol 15 mg

# 145-Chunky Tomato Cabbage Soup

**Time: 33 minutes**

**Serve: 4**

## Ingredients:

- 3 cups cabbage, chopped
- 1/2 onion, sliced
- 2 tbsp olive oil
- 6 oz tomato paste
- 13 oz can stewed tomatoes
- 4 cups of water
- 4 garlic cloves, diced
- 14 oz can tomatoes, diced
- 1/4 tsp pepper
- 1 1/2 tsp salt

## Directions:

- Heat oil in a pan over medium heat.
- Add onion and garlic and sauté for 2 minutes. Transfer to the soup maker.

- Add remaining ingredients to the soup maker and stir well.
- Seal soup maker with lid and cook on chunky mode for 28 minutes.
- Season with salt and pepper.
- Serve and enjoy.

**Nutritional Value (Amount per Serving):**

- Calories 162
- Fat 7 g
- Carbohydrates 22 g
- Sugar 12 g
- Protein 4 g
- Cholesterol 16 mg

# 146-Italian Cabbage Soup

**Time: 33 minutes**

**Serve: 4**

### Ingredients:

- 1/2 cabbage head, chopped
- 1 tsp Creole seasoning
- 1 tsp Italian seasoning
- 4 cups chicken broth
- 1 bell pepper, diced
- 3 celery ribs, diced
- 2 cups mixed salad greens
- 2 leeks, chopped
- 1 garlic clove, minced
- 2 carrots, diced
- Pepper
- Salt

## Directions:

- Add all ingredients except salad greens into the soup maker and stir well.
- Seal soup maker with lid and cook on chunky mode for 28 minutes.
- Add salad greens and stir well.
- Serve and enjoy.

## Nutritional Value (Amount per Serving):

- Calories 190
- Fat 9 g
- Carbohydrates 20 g
- Sugar 8 g
- Protein 8 g
- Cholesterol 13 mg

# 147-White Bean Carrot Soup

**Time: 38 minutes**

**Serve: 4**

## Ingredients:

- 14 oz can white beans, rinsed and drained
- 3 cups chicken stock
- 1 garlic cloves, minced
- 1 onion, diced
- 2 tbsp olive oil
- 14 oz can tomatoes crushed, drained
- 1 carrot, diced
- 2 celery stalks, diced
- Pepper
- Salt

## Directions:

- Heat oil in a pan over medium heat.
- Add onion, carrot, garlic, and celery and sauté until softened. Transfer to the soup maker.

- Add remaining ingredients to the soup maker and stir well.
- Seal soup maker with lid and cook on chunky mode for 28 minutes.
- Season soup with salt and pepper.
- Serve and enjoy.

**Nutritional Value (Amount per Serving):**

- Calories 290
- Fat 8.4 g
- Carbohydrates 46 g
- Sugar 3 g
- Protein 12 g
- Cholesterol 10 mg

# 148-Curried Cauliflower Soup

**Time: 30 minutes**

**Serve: 4**

**Ingredients:**

- 2 cups cauliflower florets
- 1 1/3 tbsp curry powder
- 2/3 cup carrots, diced
- 1 cup onion, diced
- 1 1/3 tbsp olive oil
- 2/3 cup cashews, chopped
- 9 oz can coconut milk
- 2 2/3 cups vegetable broth
- 1/8 tsp thyme
- 1/8 tsp pepper
- 1/8 tsp salt

## Directions:

- Heat oil in a pan over medium heat.
- Add carrots, onion, and cauliflower and sauté for 5 minutes. Transfer to the soup maker.
- Add remaining ingredients except for coconut milk and cashews to the soup maker and stir well.
- Seal soup maker with lid and cook on smooth mode for 21 minutes.
- Add coconut milk and stir well.
- Top with chopped cashews and serve.

## Nutritional Value (Amount per Serving):

- Calories 360
- Fat 30 g
- Carbohydrates 17 g
- Sugar 5 g
- Protein 8 g
- Cholesterol 0 mg

# 149-Healthy Tomato Green Bean Soup

**Time: 38 minutes**

**Serve: 4**

## Ingredients:

- 1/2 lb green beans, cut into 1-inch pieces
- 1/2 tsp dried basil
- 1 1/2 cup tomatoes, diced
- 1 garlic clove, minced
- 3 1/2 cups vegetable stock
- 1 tbsp butter
- 1/2 cup carrots, chopped
- 1/2 cup onion, chopped
- Pepper
- Salt

## Directions:

- Melt butter in a pan over medium heat.
- Add onion and carrot and sauté for 5 minutes. Transfer to the soup maker.

- Add remaining ingredients to the soup maker and stir well.
- Seal soup maker with lid and cook on chunky mode for 28 minutes.
- Season soup with salt and pepper.
- Serve and enjoy.

**Nutritional Value (Amount per Serving):**

- Calories 70
- Fat 3.6 g
- Carbohydrates 10.1 g
- Sugar 4.4 g
- Protein 2 g
- Cholesterol 8 mg

# 150-Almond Green Bean Soup

**Time: 30 minutes**

**Serve: 4**

## Ingredients:

- 1 lb green beans, chopped
- 4 cups vegetable stock
- 2 carrots, peeled and chopped
- 1 garlic clove, crushed
- 2 onions, chopped
- 3 tbsp olive oil
- 1/2 cup almond flour
- Pepper
- Salt

## Directions:

- Heat oil in a pan over medium heat.
- Add onion, carrots, and garlic and sauté until onion is softened. Transfer to the soup maker.

- Add remaining ingredients except almond flour to the soup maker and stir well.
- Seal soup maker with lid and cook on smooth mode for 21 minutes.
- Add almond flour and stir everything well.
- Season soup with salt and pepper.
- Serve and enjoy.

**Nutritional Value (Amount per Serving):**

- Calories 243
- Fat 18 g
- Carbohydrates 20 g
- Sugar 6 g
- Protein 6 g
- Cholesterol 0 mg

# Conclusion:

Soups are not only delicious, they also contain essential vitamins such as vitamin A, vitamin C, vitamin D, nutrients and fibers. They help to boost your energy levels because they contain carbohydrates, proteins, and nutrients. Soups are easily digested and provide a steady source of energy to your body. In this soup maker cookbook, you will have found 150 healthy, delicious and nutritious soup recipes.

Thank you for downloading this book! I hope you found the recipes as delicious and mouth-watering as I did.

Happy Cooking!

Printed in Poland
by Amazon Fulfillment
Poland Sp. z o.o., Wrocław